A Guided Journal to Build Self Confidence in the Mentally Ill

By Rebecca Chamaa

Eliezer Tristan Publishing
Portland, OR

Cover design by Aaron Smith

A Guided Journal to Build Self Confidence in the Mentally Ill

Because of the stigma and misconceptions surrounding mental illness, receiving a diagnosis of one can cause the person who is diagnosed to take a huge hit to their self-confidence.

I have schizophrenia and I am constantly exposed (especially through social media) to derogatory statements about my diagnosis. I'm not alone though; almost everyone with a mental illness must wade through stereotypes and negative comments daily. I started using guided journals to increase my gratitude and productivity almost a year ago. I have seen dramatic change in my life by creating a morning writing routine (positive thought routine) around the guided journals I use.

This journal - the one you are holding in your hands - was created specifically for those battling mental illness. It is set up to assign a task every day for 60 days. After most tasks, there will be two blank pages for you to complete the task on. Some tasks have other directions that don't require added pages.

After you finish the journal, I hope you will take another 60 days to go back through it and add to your original responses. Have things changed? Do you feel more grounded? Do you feel better about yourself?

Before getting into the first task, let me leave you with something I believe: you are wild and wonderful, your creativity is without boundaries, and the lack of walls around your imagination is your superpower! Let's get going!

Day 1:

Write down all the things you are good at. You can include folding t-shirts or playing scrabble! Try to think of at least five things and add to this list as often as possible.

_____

_____

_____

_____

_____

_____

_____

_____

_____

_____

_____

_____

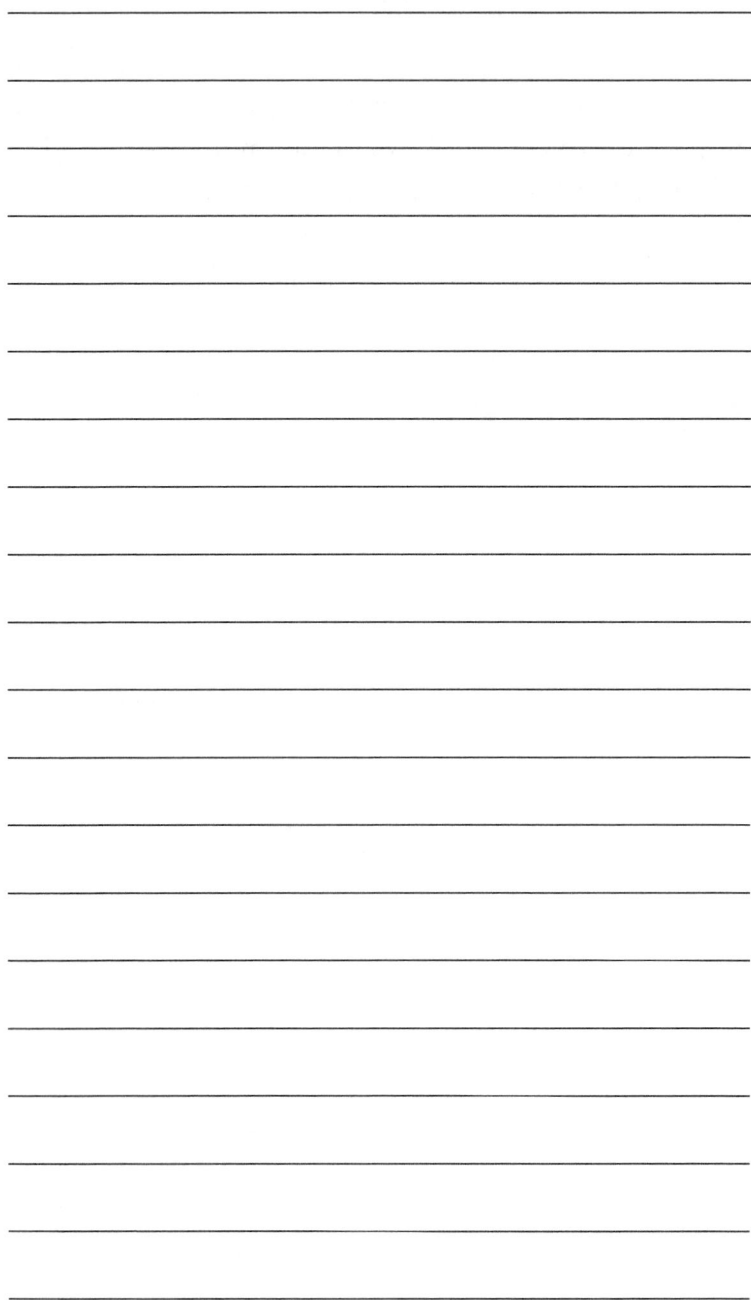

Day 2:

Write down all the things you dream of doing. You can include the simple to the extravagant - from cleaning your room to traveling to the Great Pyramids to writing a book.

_____

_____

_____

_____

_____

_____

_____

_____

_____

_____

_____

_____

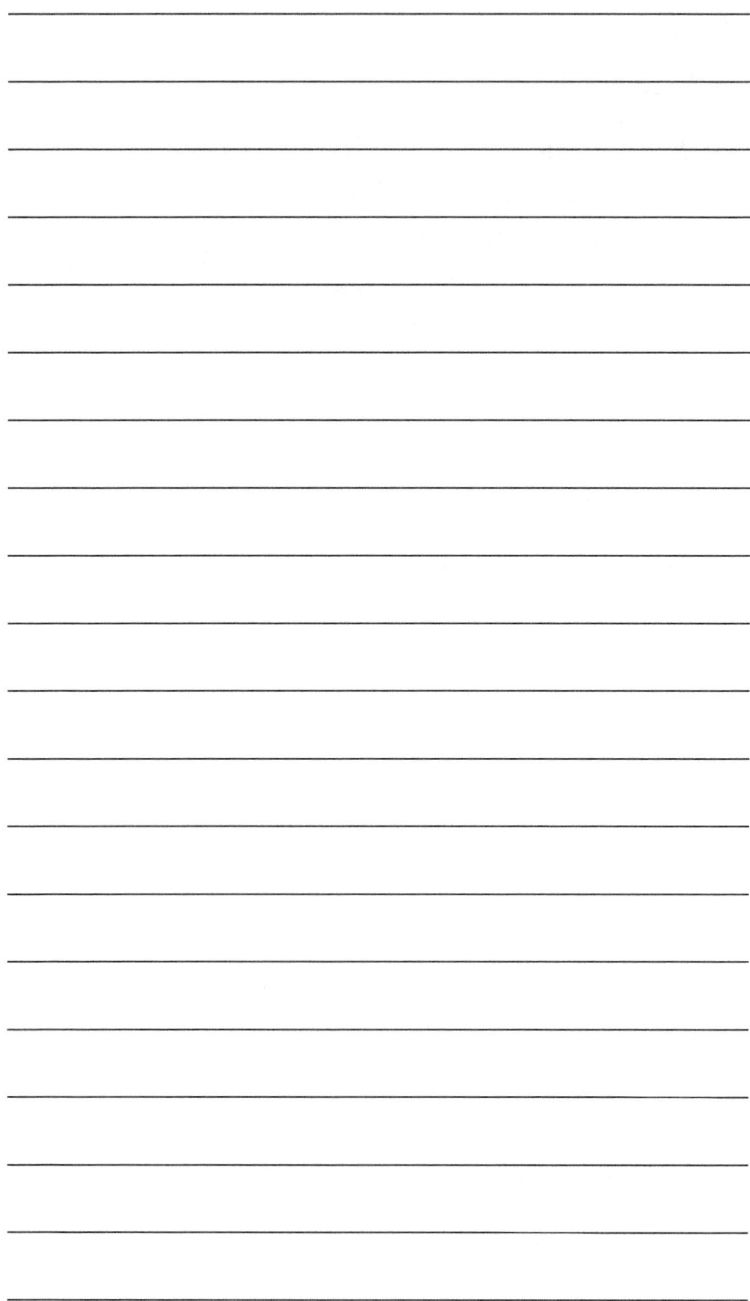

Day 3:

Look over your list from Day 2. Are there any steps you can take today to work toward your dreams? Write the dream here and think of two to three manageable steps you can start taking today to make the dream a reality.

If your dream is to write a novel or memoir, take a free class online to learn more about the craft of writing. If you have an idea for a book, list the chapters and start to map it out. If your dream is to buy the latest iPhone or visit the city of your dreams, find a jar and start putting your change in it, saved from skipping coffee or having lunch out. Those dollars will add up over time. Try an app on your phone that helps you save spare change like Acorns.

Whatever your dream is, think of the steps needed to make it happen! Every step taken is going forward. Going forward builds momentum. Keep moving!

_____

_____

_____

_____

_____

_____

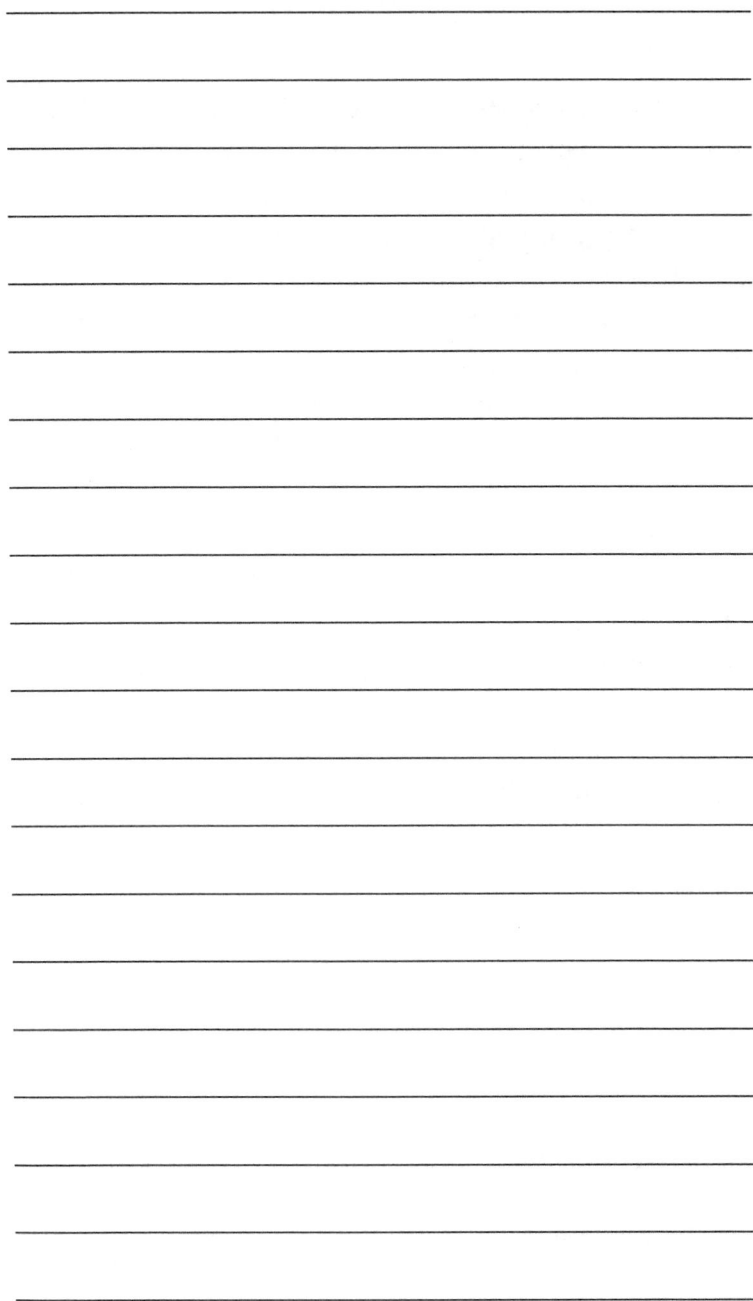

Day 4:

Use the computer or go to the library and make a list of successful people who have the same illness that you do. Using Google, you can type in, "famous people with bipolar" or "famous people with schizophrenia" or "famous people with OCD." You might have to do some digging to find people with your disorder, but if you try different combinations of words, you will find results - and hopefully, you are encouraged and surprised by what others have managed to accomplish. The next person on the list could be you!

_____

_____

_____

_____

_____

_____

_____

_____

Day 5:

Make a list of things you loved while growing up. Make sure to include things that brought you comfort. For example, peanut butter and jelly sandwiches, a favorite television show, a book, etc.

_____

_____

_____

_____

_____

_____

_____

_____

_____

_____

_____

_____

Day 6:

Look at the list from Day 5. What can you do in your daily life to recreate those experiences that once brought comfort to you? For example, if you loved a particular blanket, do you still have it? If not, can you buy one that you think you could learn to love (maybe a weighted blanket or a handmade quilt) and use it to comfort you?

I curl up under a quilt every morning and complete my morning writing routine. Now, when I am sick, or feeling unwell, I want that quilt on top of me. It has become a source of comfort to me.

Create an environment for yourself where you have several sources of comfort. Even if it means eating a peanut butter and jelly sandwich every day at noon.

Day 7:

Make a list of nice things people have said to you. It can be a parent, a teacher, a neighbor, or anyone else you have encountered. If you can't think of any nice things people have said to you, write a list of things you wish people would have said to you – the things you needed to hear growing up or things you need to hear today.

_____

_____

_____

_____

_____

_____

_____

_____

_____

_____

_____

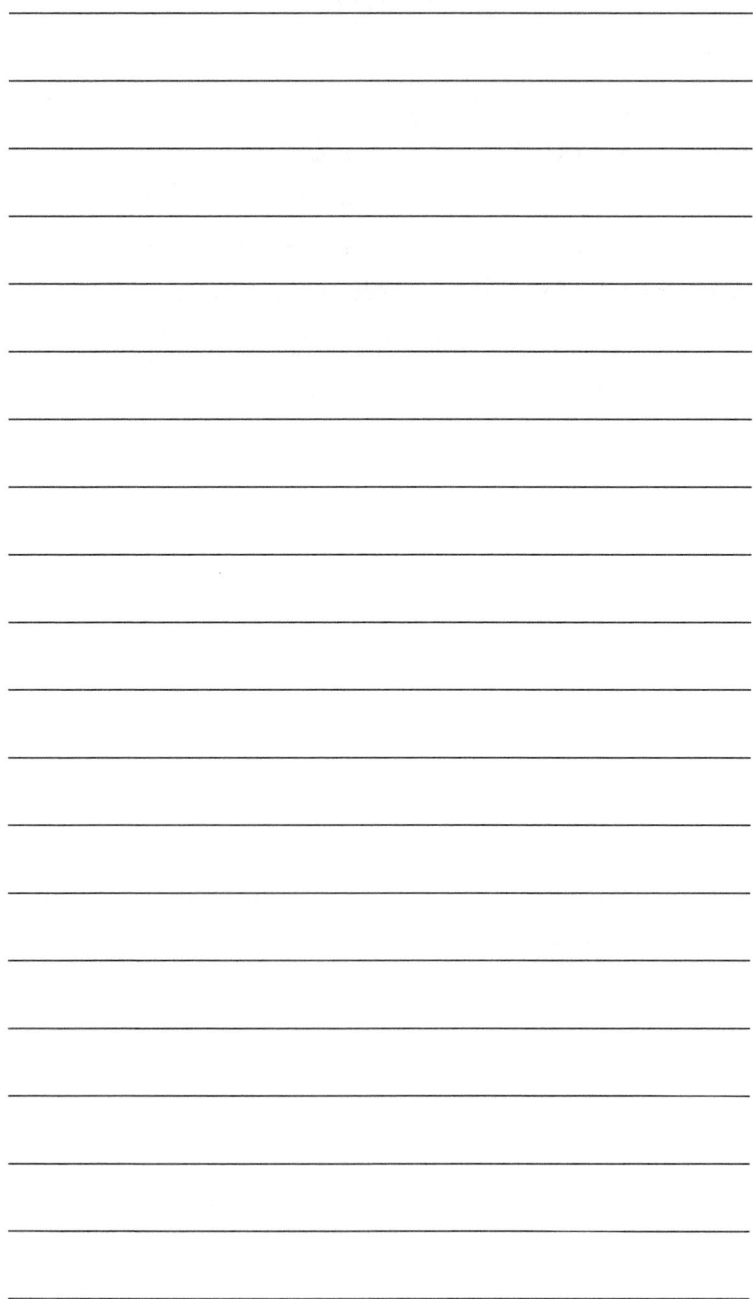

Day 8:

List all the nice things you can remember doing for others.

_____

_____

_____

_____

_____

_____

_____

_____

_____

_____

_____

_____

_____

_____

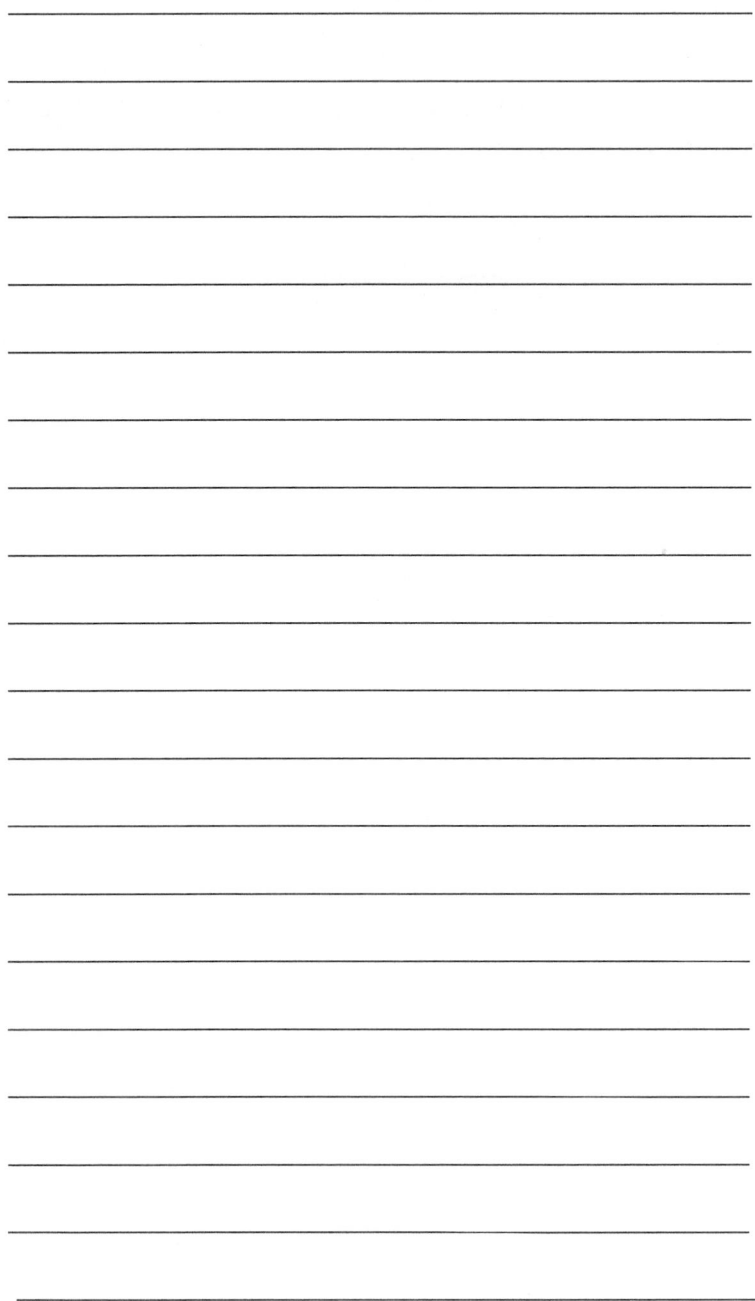

Day 9:

Write down all the qualities you love in other people. Put a check mark beside those qualities that also describe you.

_____

_____

_____

_____

_____

_____

_____

_____

_____

_____

_____

_____

_____

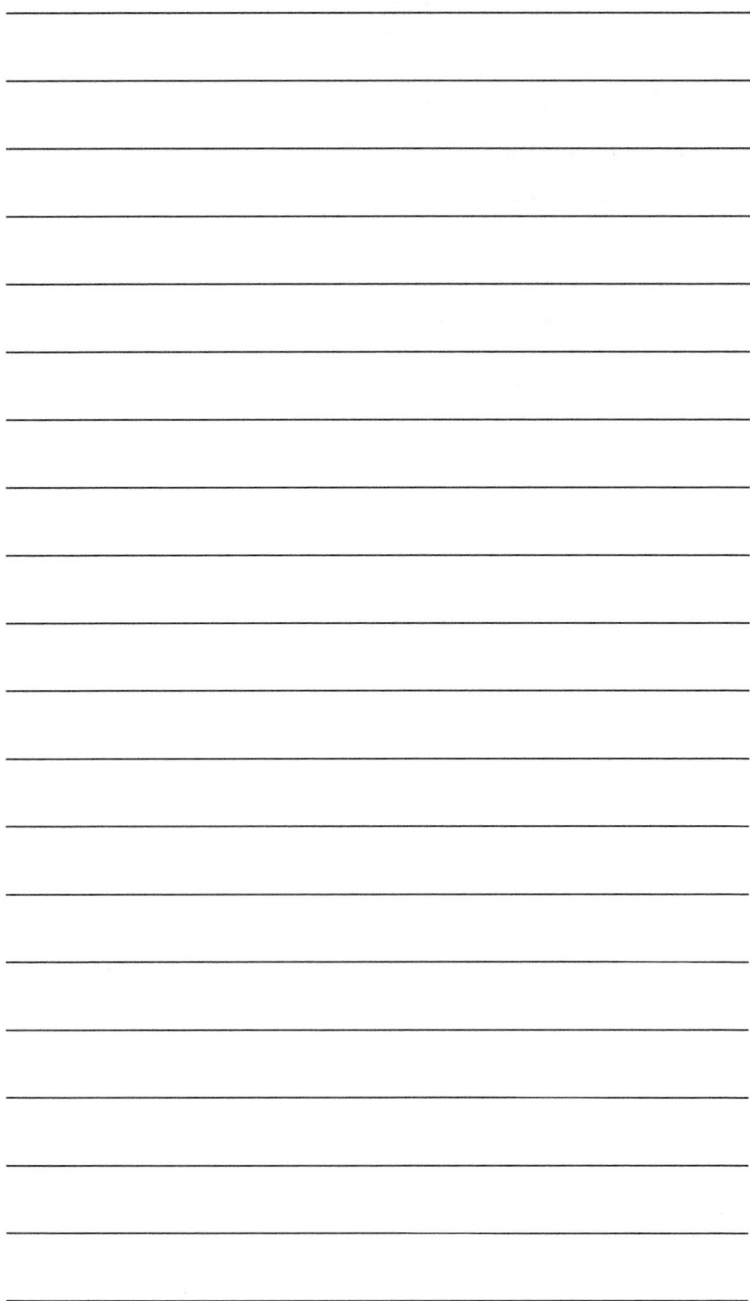

Day 10:

Try to remember a time in your life that you were the happiest. What made you happy? What is different now? Write it. Is it possible to bring some of that happiness back by doing things you did then?

_____

_____

_____

_____

_____

_____

_____

_____

_____

_____

_____

_____

_____

_____

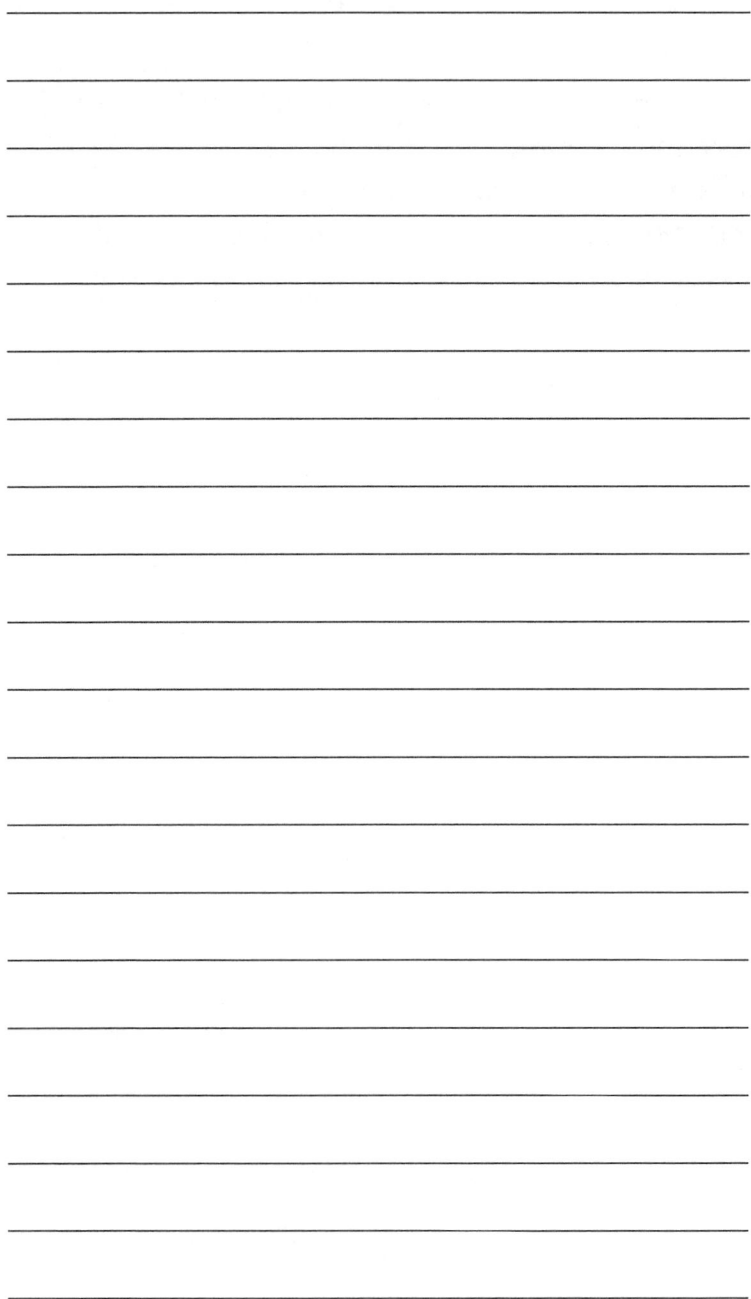

Day 11:

List quick (5 minute) tasks that you can complete every day. Try to complete one or two of them each day.

I make my bed, do the dishes, unload the dish washer, clean the mirrors, throw out the trash, or dust my workspace. These are the small tasks that help me feel like I have accomplished something.

Making a list of tasks and checking them off can boost your mood.

_____

_____

_____

_____

_____

_____

_____

_____

_____

_____

_____

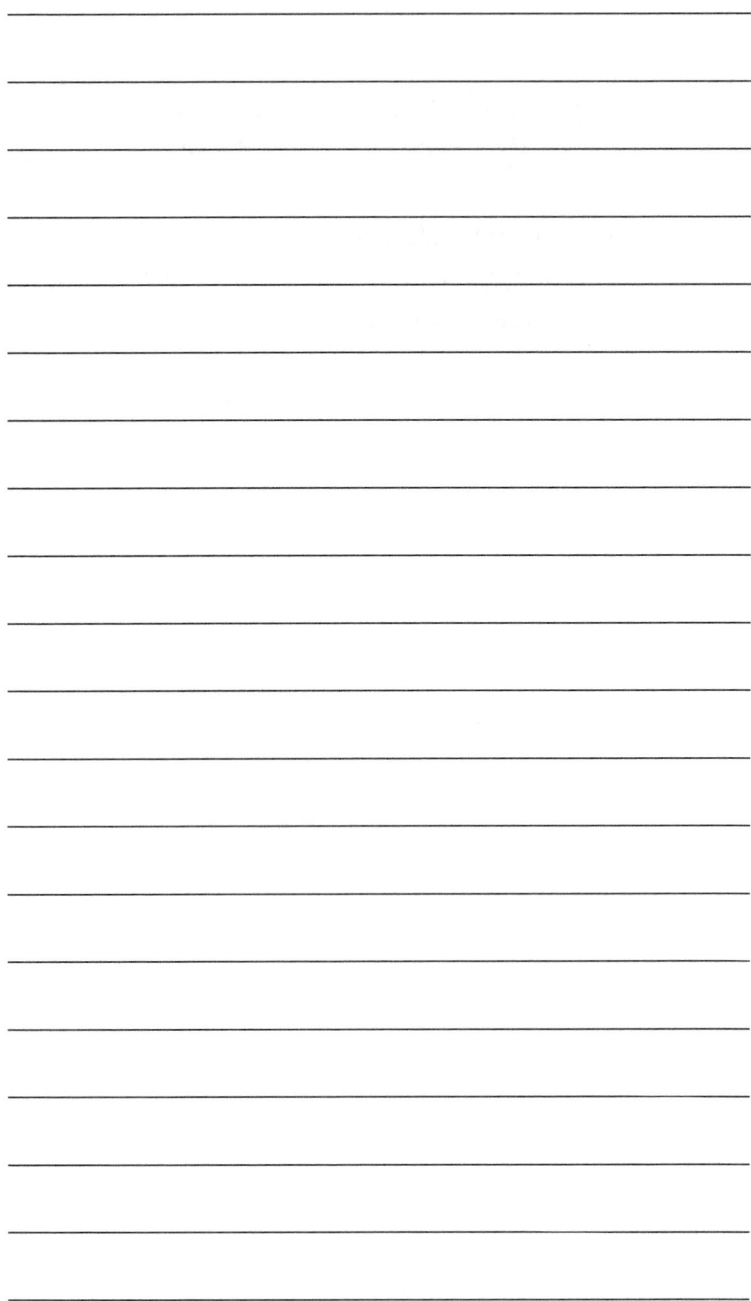

Day 12:

Find a quote online or in a book that encourages you. Write the quote on a piece of paper and tape it near your desk, on your mirror or on your refrigerator – anywhere where you can see it daily.

The quote on my desk is by Katie Doucette, it says, "Every day write down the good stuff. Read it back and you will see a wonderful life."

Day 13:

On the next two pages, write the sentence, "I am loved," as many times as you can. Use both the front and the back. Fill every inch of white space with these three words.

_____

_____

_____

_____

_____

_____

_____

_____

_____

_____

_____

_____

_____

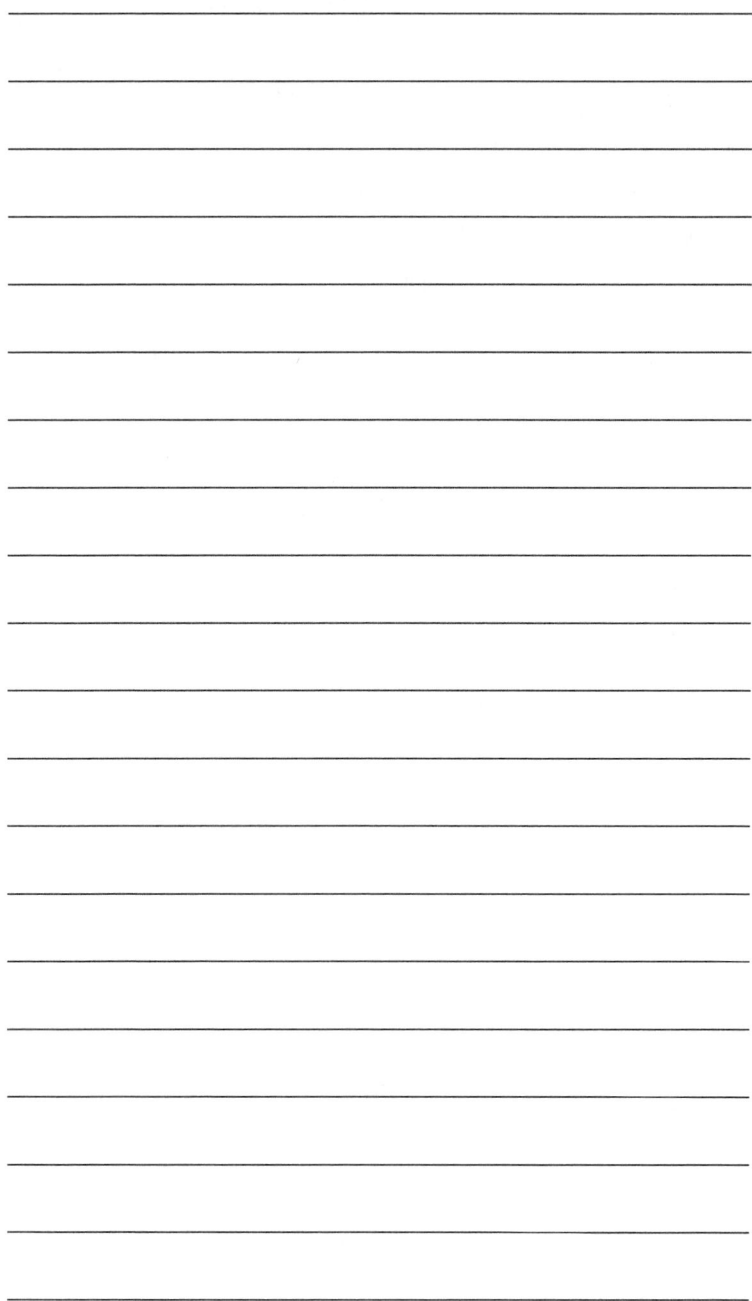

Day 14:

Go through photographs of yourself, either digitally or in print, and pick 4-6 of them to put up near your desk or on your refrigerator. Choose pictures where you think you look your best, you are with someone you love, you are the happiest, etc.

I have pictures of my husband and I when we were younger, and other pictures when we were making silly faces at each other. These images remind me that my life has had some wonderful, fun, meaningful, joyous moments. Great moments are not all behind me, they can and will come again.

Day 15:

Read an essay from the *New Yorker* or NYT's Modern Love. The goal is to read an essay that is well-written and takes you out of yourself for ten to fifteen minutes.

If you don't have internet access (these magazines and papers have an online version), take a trip to the library or the bookstore and find material that you can read. Let writers take you to a world outside of your own.

Day 16:

Read a poem or two.

Poets who I recommend are Mary Oliver, Sharon Olds, Billy Collins, Dorianne Laux… but you can also find one on your own!

Let the words, images and mood of the poem inspire you. Then try to write a poem of your own.

Day 17:

Make a list of things that make your life easier.
One big thing on my list is my refrigerator!
Imagine living life without refrigeration.

_____

_____

_____

_____

_____

_____

_____

_____

_____

_____

_____

_____

_____

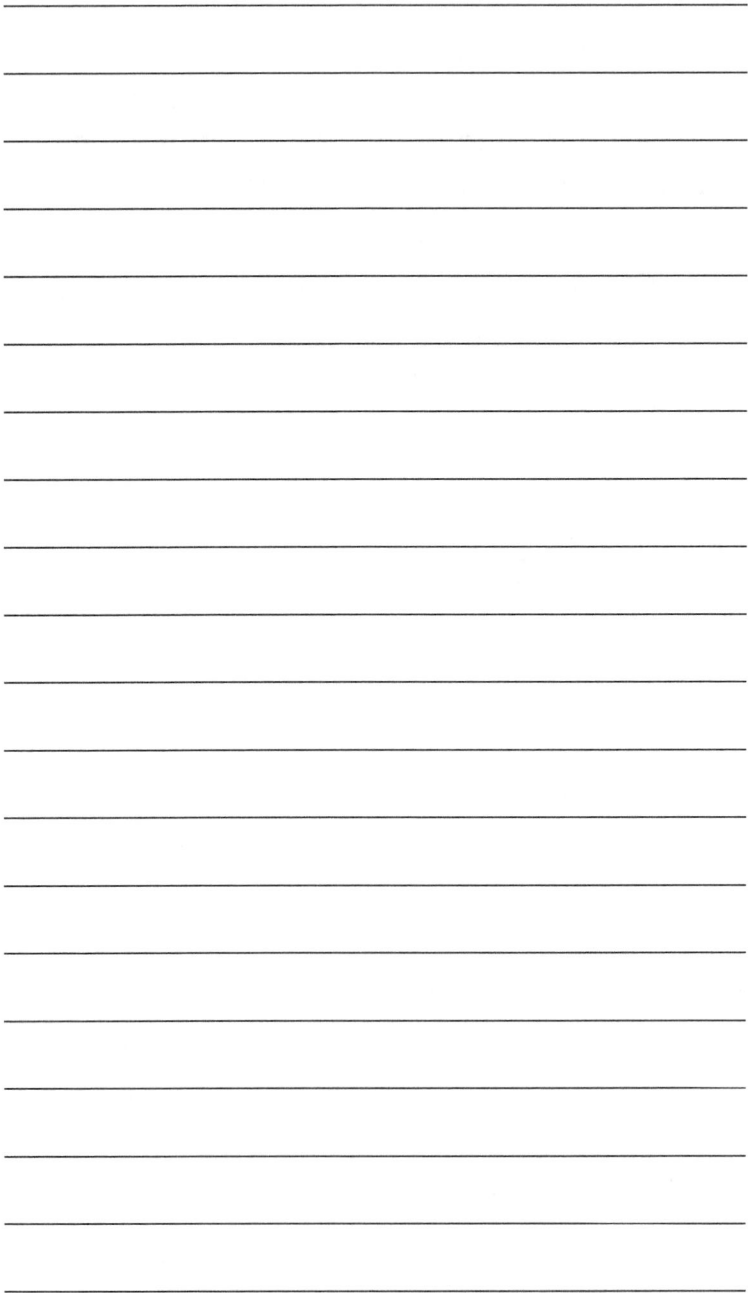

Day 18:

Write down all your favorite foods. Underline the ones that are healthy. Try to work all the healthy foods that you love into your diet regularly. Not only will you feel satisfied by eating some of your favorite foods, but you will feel good about your choices.

Some of my favorites are cantaloupe, applesauce (unsweetened with a dash of cinnamon), beans, and mashed sweet potatoes.

_____

_____

_____

_____

_____

_____

_____

_____

_____

_____

_____

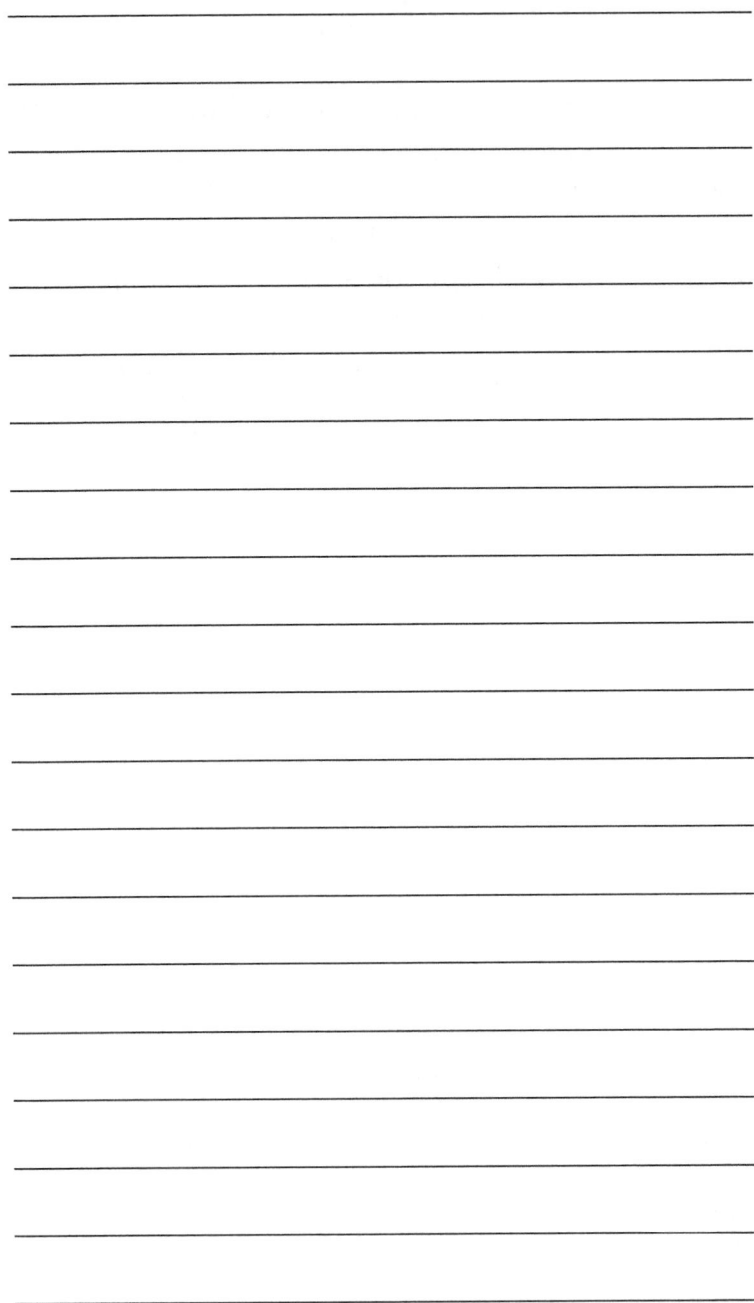

Day 19:

Buy a sketchbook and doodle for fifteen minutes, three to five times a week (the more the better).

I am not a good artist (that isn't the point), but I doodle all the time. I often look at faces of famous people and draw them in all-green or all-purple or blue.

Get creative. Add words if you want, glue on bubble gum wrappers or pictures from magazines. The goal is to create and do it without judgement. Your creations are neither good nor bad – they are the oil that gets your imagination working. Do this as often as you can.

Day 20:

If you have time this week (and the resources), bake or cook something. It can be as simple as a box cake or as elaborate as a five-course meal. It doesn't matter if it has three ingredients! The point is to make something that can nurture you. Creating in the kitchen not only gives us a sense of accomplishment, it is using our imagination to feed ourselves.

Day 21:

Go to a website like Highbrow and sign up for one of their free classes. Highbrow classes come in your e-mail every morning and only take about five minutes each day. If you have more than five to ten minutes a day, search for other free classes online. Some major universities offer select classes for free, and plenty of those are writing classes if that interests you.

Day 22:

Think of the best period of your life. Try to recall five to ten bands or songs from that time. Find those bands or songs on YouTube and listen to a few of them. If you want, write down some of the memories these songs bring back to you.

_____

_____

_____

_____

_____

_____

_____

_____

_____

_____

_____

_____

_____

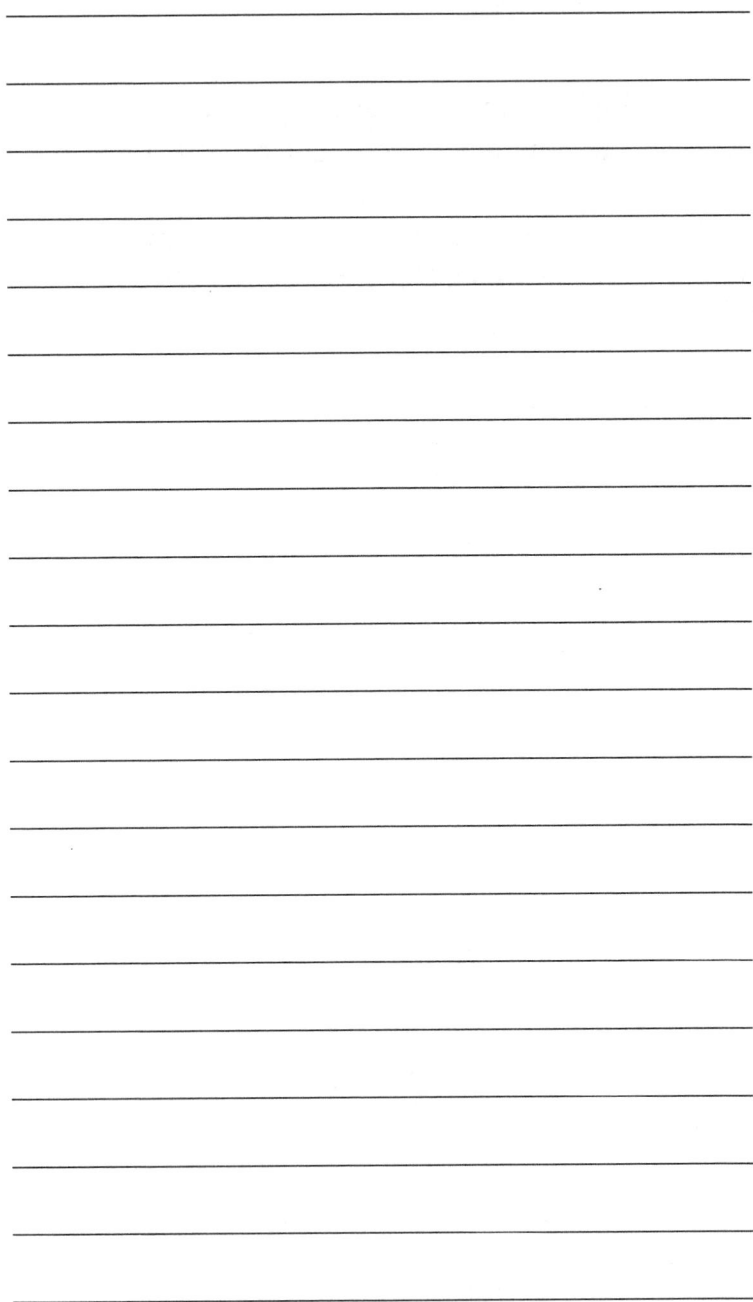

Day 23:

    Think about your proudest moment. That moment can be anything from graduating school, getting an A on an exam, finishing an eight-hundred-page book, making a touchdown, or something like learning to swim. Write down the steps you took to make that moment happen. Is there anything you can do to apply those steps to a current dream of yours to move it closer to fruition?

    After two years of goofing off, I started getting straight A's in college. It took a lot of time and effort to get high marks. When I apply that time and effort to projects I want to succeed today, the results are always satisfying.

_____

_____

_____

_____

_____

_____

_____

_____

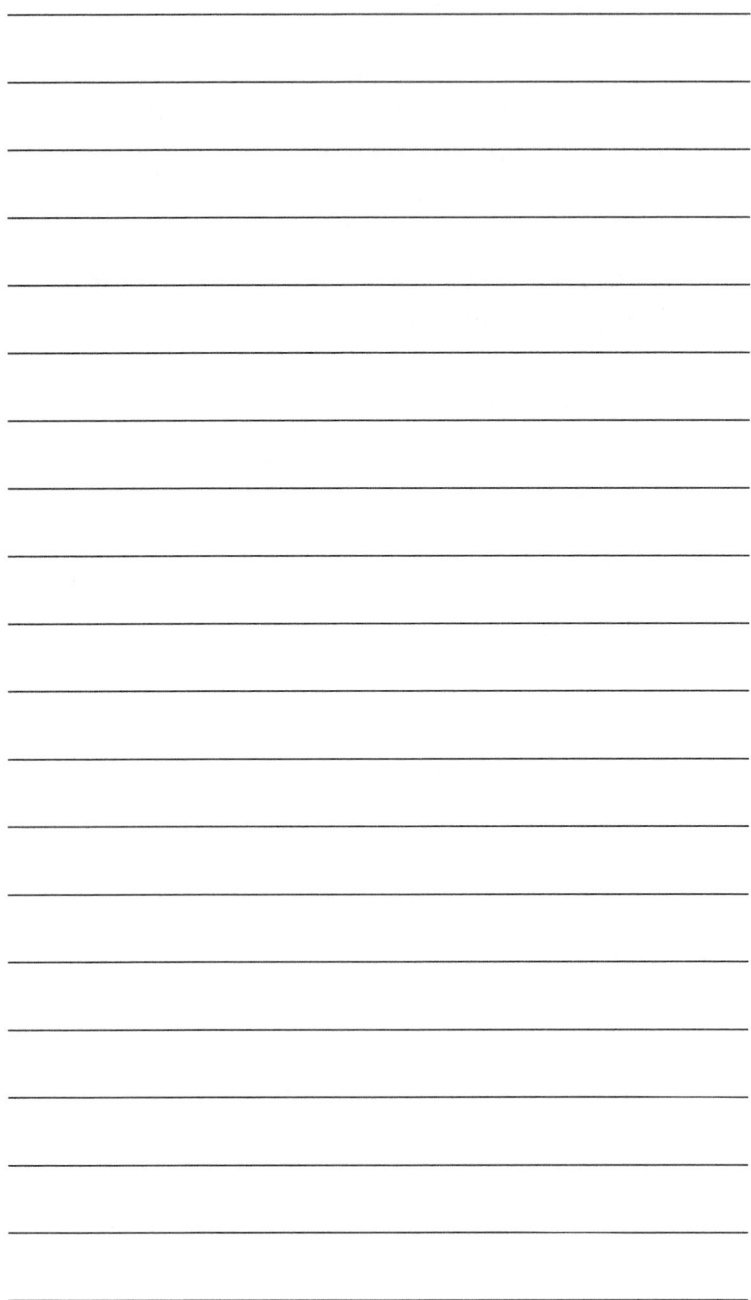

Day 24:

Go to YouTube and watch one episode of a show you loved as a child.

Day 25:

Write a list of your favorite teachers, mentors and/or coaches. Write one to two paragraphs (or sentences) about why they were your favorite.

_____

_____

_____

_____

_____

_____

_____

_____

_____

_____

_____

_____

_____

Day 26:

    Do something new today. It can be as simple as reading a new poem, or it could be trying a new recipe (bread is not that hard and super therapeutic to make). Maybe try a new coffee shop! Use your imagination – shake things up in your day.

Day 27:

Make a card for someone you love. Use whatever you have around the house (some ideas are wallpaper, magazines, colored pencils, tape, glue, etc.). If you want, you can send the card to that person (if they are still alive and you have contact with them). Getting postal mail is fun because so much of our lives are lived online these days. A handmade card is special. There is no need to send it though, it is the process of making it that matters.

Day 28:

Make a list of people you can count on no matter what. If you don't have anyone, make up people that you wish you could count on. What would they be like? What would the two of you do if you could spend a day together?

Personally, the list of people I can count on is very short, so I made up some people to add to my list.

_____

_____

_____

_____

_____

_____

_____

_____

_____

_____

_____

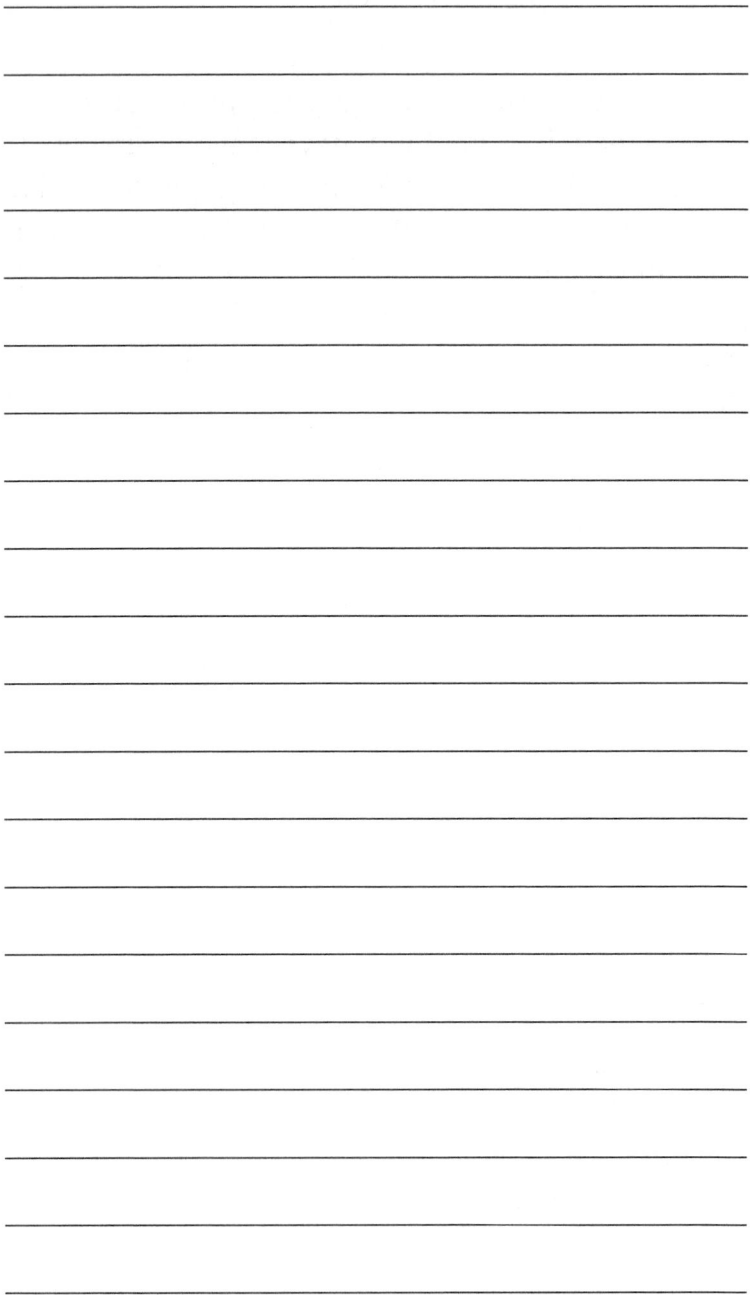

Day 29:

Draft an e-mail or letter to the people in your life who matter the most to you. Tell them the qualities they have that you admire. You can choose to send this, or not (use your discretion - you don't want to send a letter that makes someone uncomfortable). Think about the qualities you admire in people. Do they overlap? Do you share some of these qualities? What is the most important to you?

Day 30:

Pick a day this week and celebrate it as if it were a holiday. It can be Christmas, Passover, Halloween, St. Patrick's, etc. Write down why you chose this holiday and how you chose to celebrate.

_____

_____

_____

_____

_____

_____

_____

_____

_____

_____

_____

_____

_____

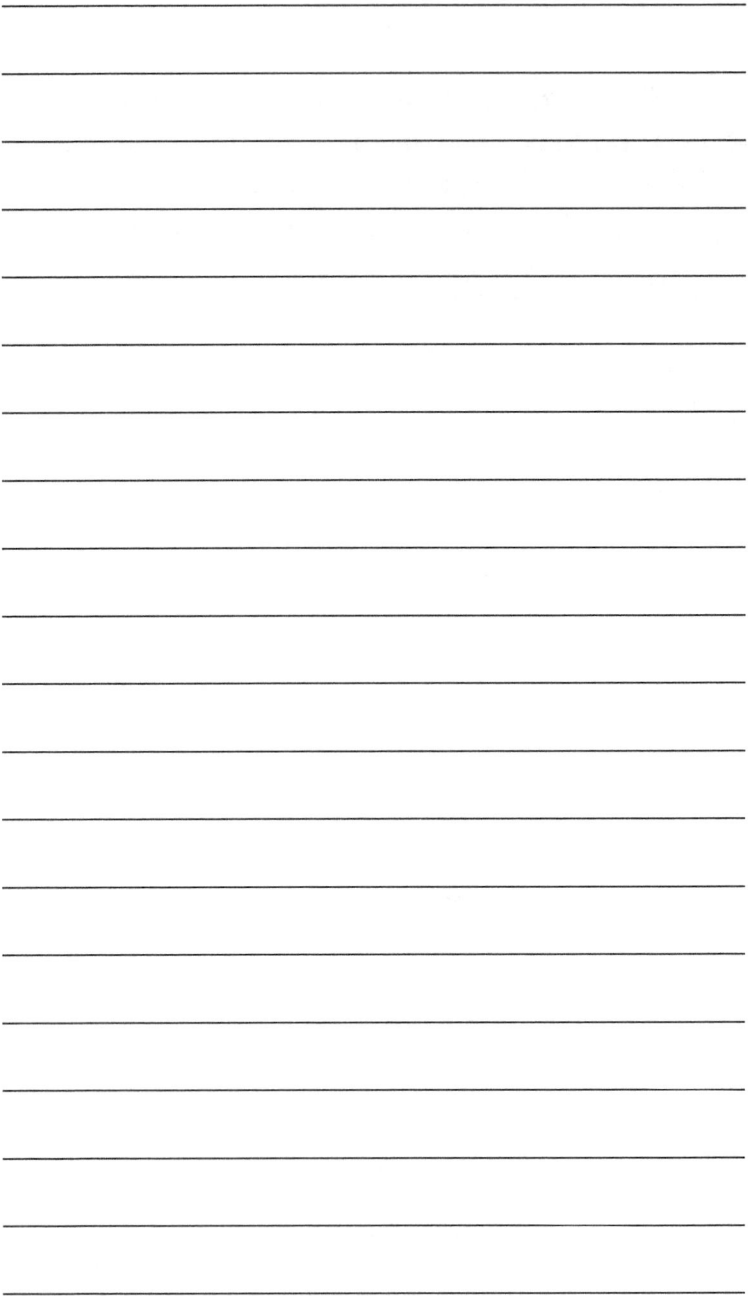

Day 31:

Start a morning ritual. Some people write in a journal to clear their mind every morning. Some people meditate or write a gratitude list.

While drinking my coffee every morning, I fill out my daily planner and do a couple of different guided journals.

Whatever ritual you choose, try to make it one that you will do every day, or at least five times a week, and make it an on-going practice.

Day 32:

Keep a grocery list during the week. Having a list will help save money at the grocery store if you stick to it. Plus, it will help you feel more organized and in control.

Day 33:

Get a plastic trash bag and try to fill it up with donations to a charity. You can donate dishes, books, shoes, clothes, etc. Drop the donations off and hopefully you will feel like you did a good deed and decluttered your home.

Day 34:

Go on a walk around your neighborhood. If you have a camera or your phone has a camera, take pictures of everything that stands out and catches your eye. Be camera happy!

Day 35:

Look through the pictures you took yesterday. Are there any that you think are particularly good? Do you have an eye for photographing people, houses, birds, flowers? Write those thoughts on the following pages. Start a project or hobby of going outside a few minutes every day or even once a week to snap some photos. Look online for places you can post your photos and share them with others (social media is always good).

_____

_____

_____

_____

_____

_____

_____

_____

_____

_____

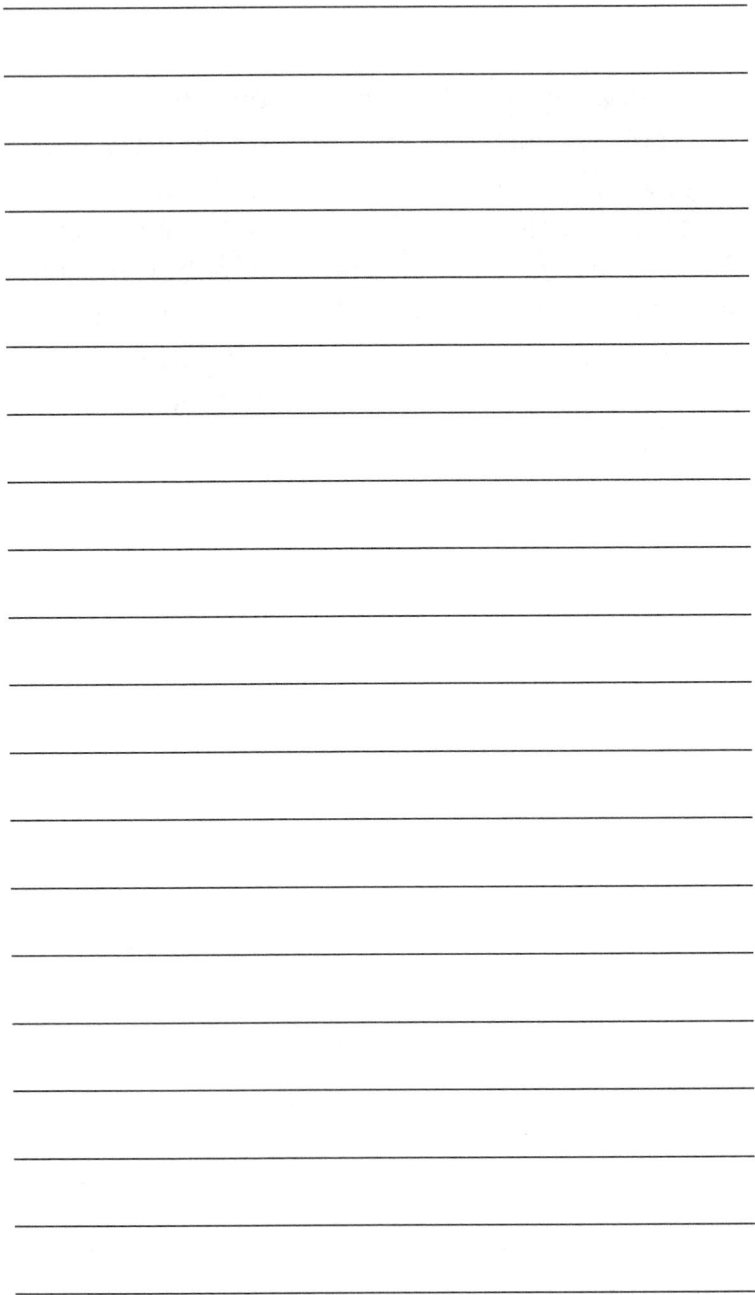

Day 36:

Write five "Facebook statuses" that you would never post but would love to. They can be funny, angry, revealing, telling a secret, or a dream you wish would come true. The act of writing something can often make one feel better, even if no one sees it.

_____

_____

_____

_____

_____

_____

_____

_____

_____

_____

_____

_____

_____

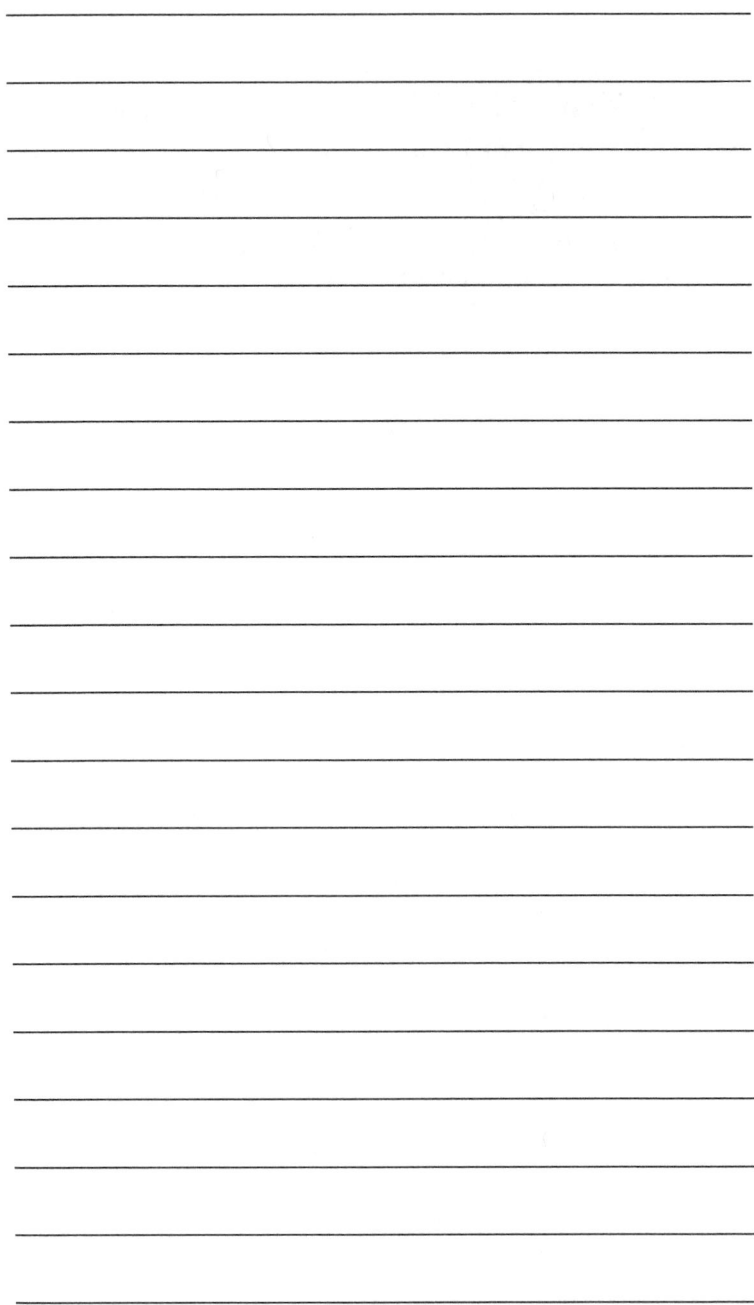

Day 37:

Write a list of the things in your life you are most grateful for. They can be things, people or events. They could have happened when you were five, ten, or fifty.

_____

_____

_____

_____

_____

_____

_____

_____

_____

_____

_____

_____

_____

_____

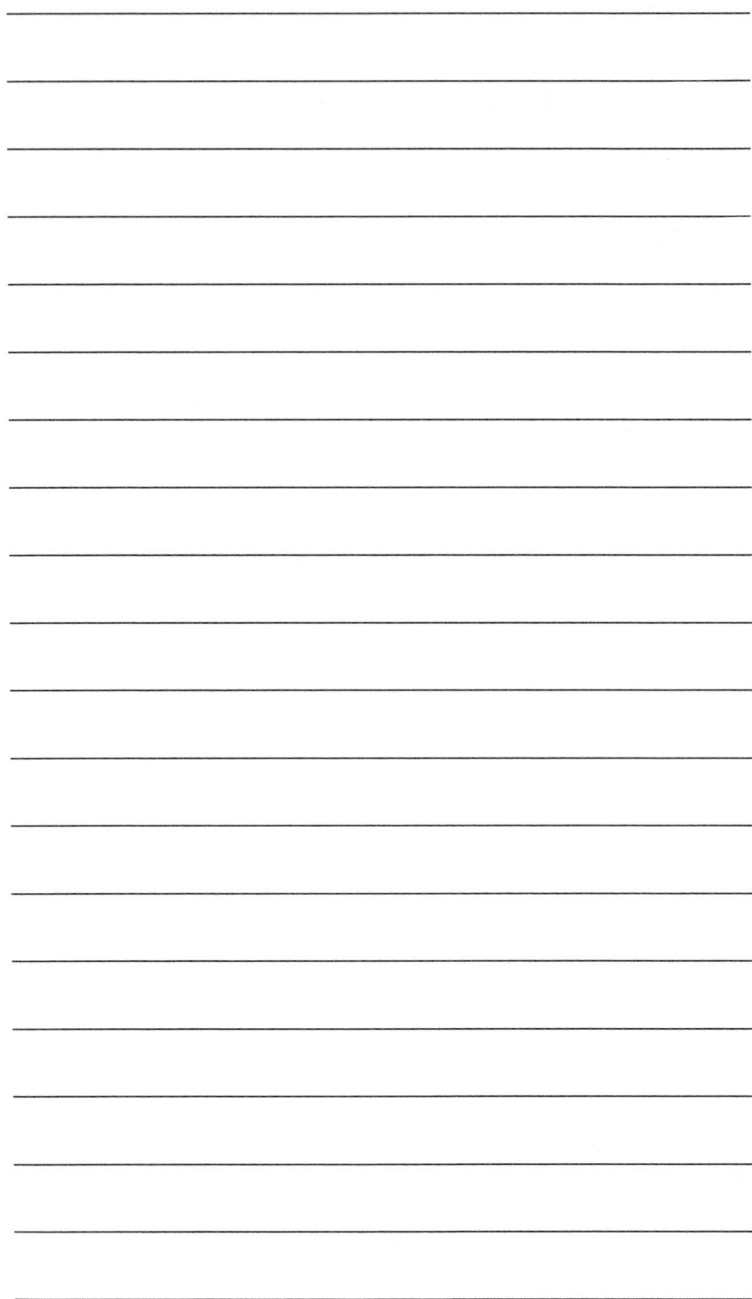

Day 38:

    Watch a comedy or standup comedian or late-night show. If you are familiar with comedians and late-night shows, watch the one that makes you laugh the most (or choose a movie that someone told you was hilarious). If you can, try to watch something that makes you laugh out loud once a week.

Day 39:

    Think of others and their needs. Let someone go in front of you in line at the grocery store, hold the door open for someone, or if you have some extra money, offer to buy a friend a coffee or ice cream cone.

Day 40:

Try to go a day without being competitive. Try not to interrupt or to have the last word in a conversation. Try to avoid games played with others. Avoid all social media if it makes you feel envious or jealous of others.

Day 41:

This one goes well with Day 40. If you are on social media, try a social media fast. Try it for a day or two, or even a week. See if you notice a change in your mood. Record how you feel about not being "connected" 24/7.

_____

_____

_____

_____

_____

_____

_____

_____

_____

_____

_____

_____

_____

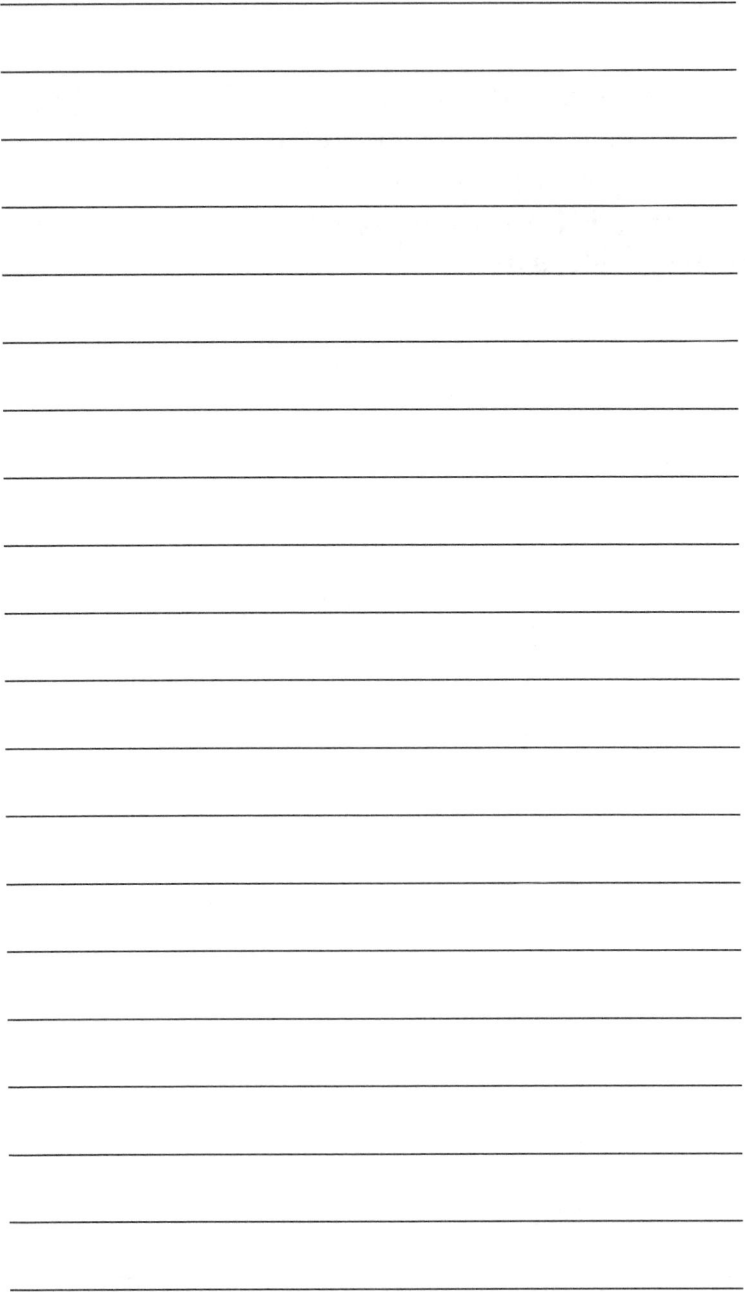

Day 42:

Try to practice your listening skills. Try to hear what others are saying. Put down your phone when you are with friends or family. Don't be quick to respond to others. Formulate your answers or response only after they have finished talking and you are certain you heard them.

Day 43:

Go through magazines and old books (Goodwill is great for buying old books) and cut out words that excite, delight, encourage, and make your imagination soar. Use a glue stick to paste the words to a piece of poster board and add to it on a regular basis. If you want, you can add pictures as well.

Day 44:

  Try to experiment in the kitchen and come up with a new recipe. It can be as simple as adding chia seeds or chocolate chips in your favorite peanut butter cookie recipe, or it can be as complicated as coming up with a vegan chili. I often create new sandwiches when I want to do something creative but don't have a lot of ingredients or energy.

_____

_____

_____

_____

_____

_____

_____

_____

_____

_____

_____

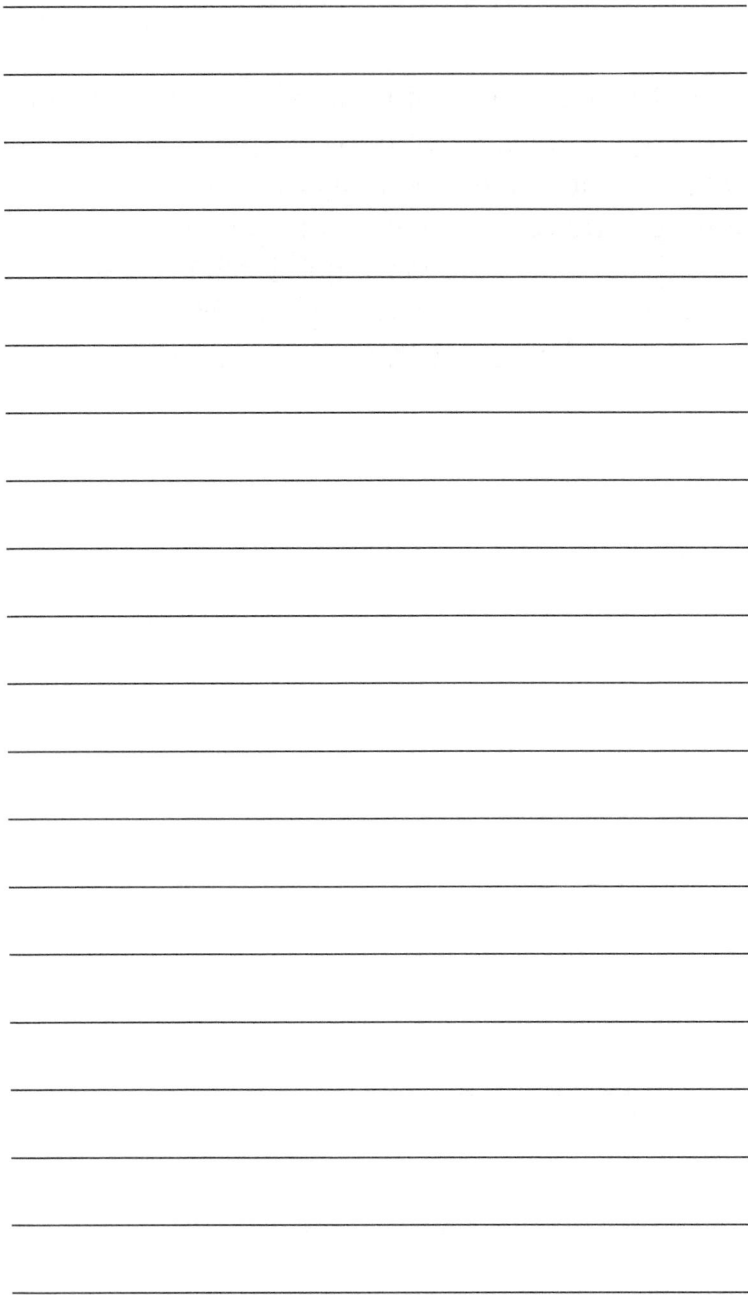

Day 45:

Spend some time with an animal. If you have pets, this is easy! If you don't, try to go to a place where people walk their dogs or visit a coffee shop that allows dogs. Make sure you are careful not to pet a dog without the owner's permission (you don't want to get bit). If you don't like dogs, or you have friends with cats, maybe you could go over for a visit.

I often go to the zoo where they allow you to pet certain animals at set times.

Day 46:

Write a paragraph selling your skills to future employers. If it takes one or two pages, that's great!

I once wrote a letter to future employers about the benefits of hiring someone with schizophrenia – it is a little bit humorous, but also true.

_____

_____

_____

_____

_____

_____

_____

_____

_____

_____

_____

_____

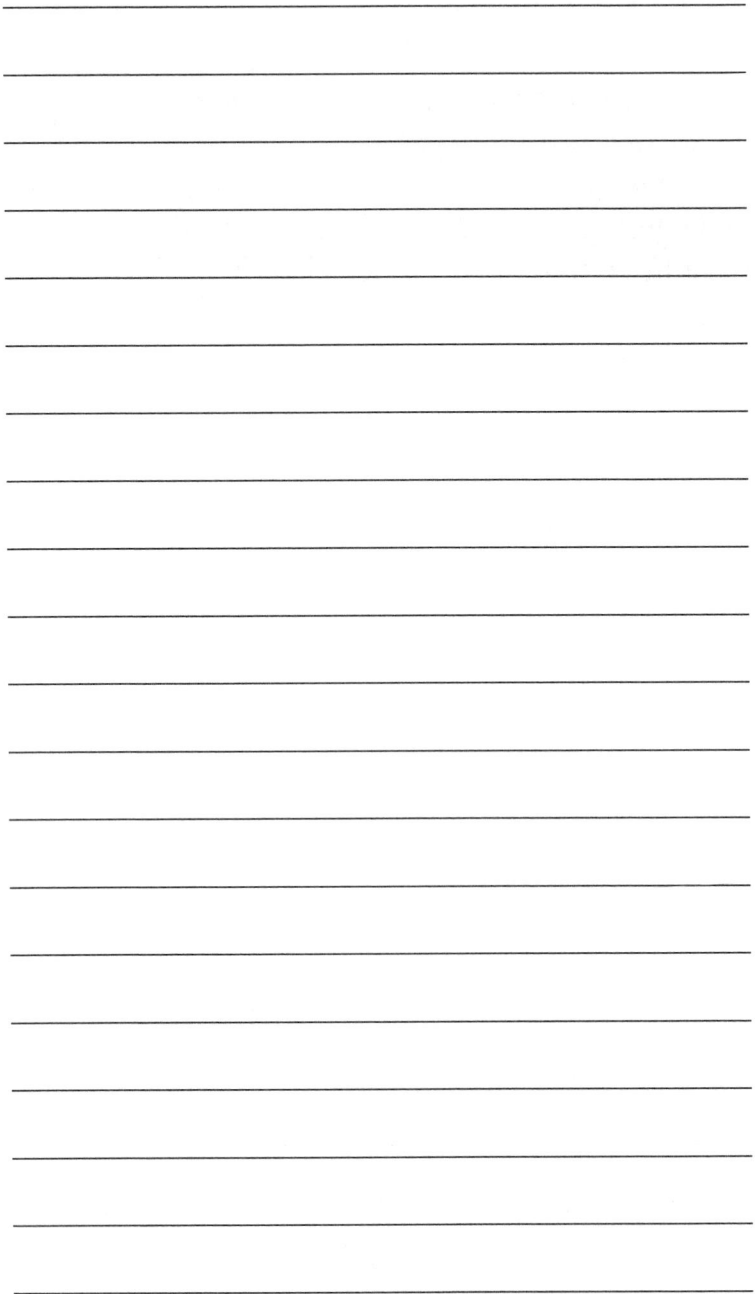

Day 47:

Pretend you are in a job interview and the interviewer asks about your strengths and weaknesses. Write an answer to the interviewer.

_____

_____

_____

_____

_____

_____

_____

_____

_____

_____

_____

_____

_____

Day 48:

Call, Skype, Messenger, etc. someone you haven't talked to in a long time but whose company you enjoy.

Day 49:

Research your city or town on the internet. Make a list of five things you would like to do even if you have done them before. Play like you are on a treasure hunt.

Every time I do this, I find new things out about my city, and make plans to do the things I have discovered.

_____

_____

_____

_____

_____

_____

_____

_____

_____

_____

_____

_____

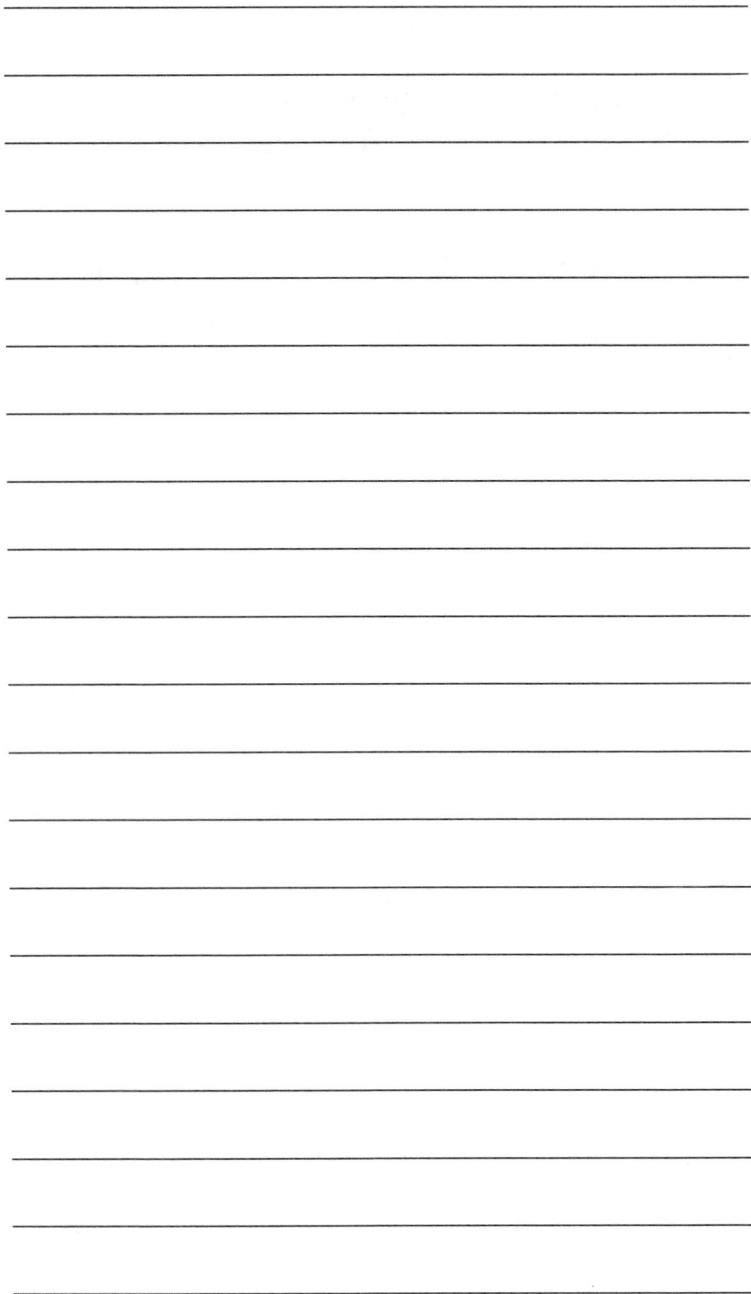

Day 50:

Offer to do something for an elderly neighbor, a new parent, or a friend. You can offer to run an errand, trim their bushes, sweep their sidewalk, walk their dog, etc.

Day 51:

Support a friend or someone in your community who has a small business. Buy something from their shop or hire them for their services. If you can't afford to buy something from their shop or pay for their services, visit their web page or store and let them know you admire their work and what they are doing. Draft them a five-star review on the next page and post it. Who knows, you might get ideas for your own business!

_____

_____

_____

_____

_____

_____

_____

_____

_____

_____

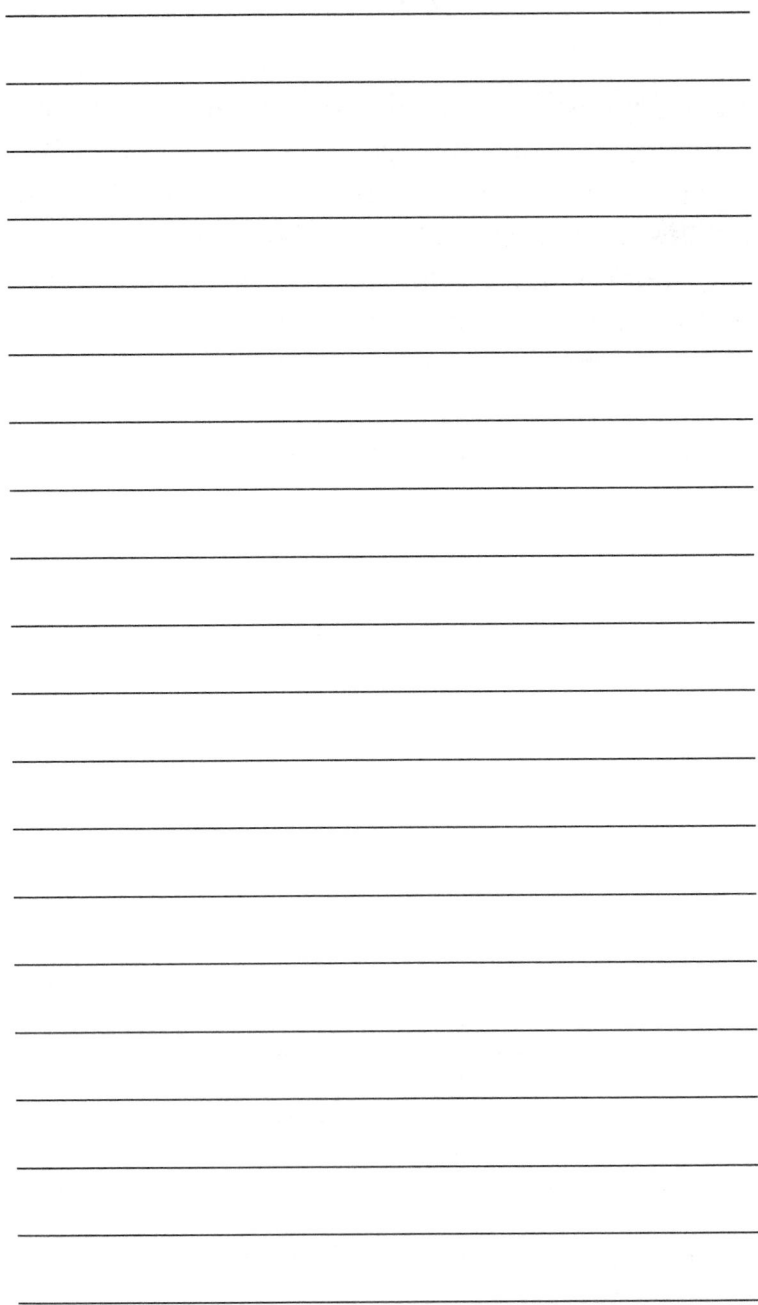

Day 52:

Brainstorm ideas for making extra money or for using your free time. You might list launching an Etsy shop, dog walking, pet sitting, grocery delivery, driving Uber or Lyft, etc.

_____

_____

_____

_____

_____

_____

_____

_____

_____

_____

_____

_____

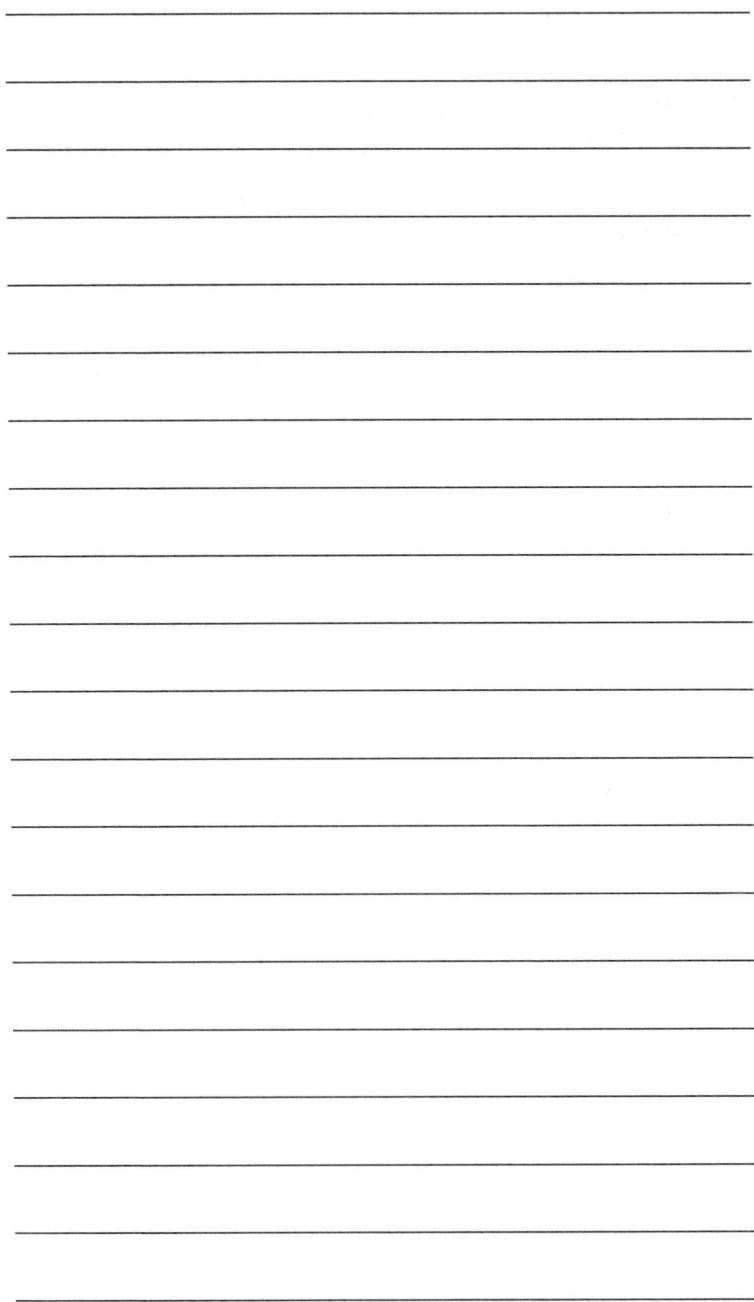

Day 53:

Write ten things that you consider self-care. For example, a manicure or pedicure, a bubble bath, a bite of chocolate cake, going to the gym, taking a walk, burning nice candles, etc. try to do one of these things every day.

_____

_____

_____

_____

_____

_____

_____

_____

_____

_____

_____

_____

_____

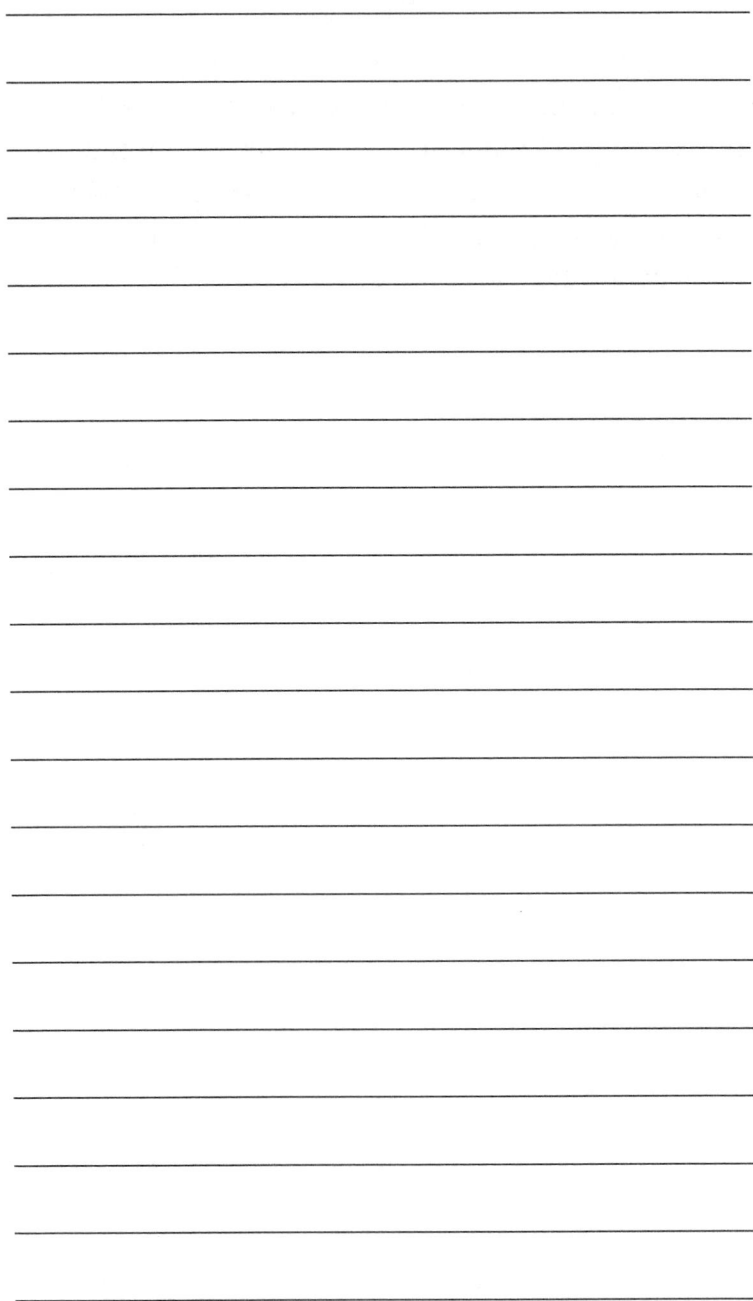

Day 54:

Try to learn a new skill by watching YouTube videos. It can be a make-up tutorial, restoring old furniture, drawing, photography, learning to knit, etc. Write a a summary of what you learned. Make a list of other things you can learn by watching YouTube videos. Try to complete your list.

_____

_____

_____

_____

_____

_____

_____

_____

_____

_____

_____

_____

Day 55:

Sing a song from beginning to end. Imagine you are in a karaoke bar preforming in front of an audience that loves you. Belt out the words! Enjoy yourself!

When I do this, I always find myself singing old love songs or songs that were popular when I was a kid.

Make a list of songs that you can remember from your childhood or teenage years. If you remember any of the lyrics, write them down.

_____

_____

_____

_____

_____

_____

_____

_____

_____

_____

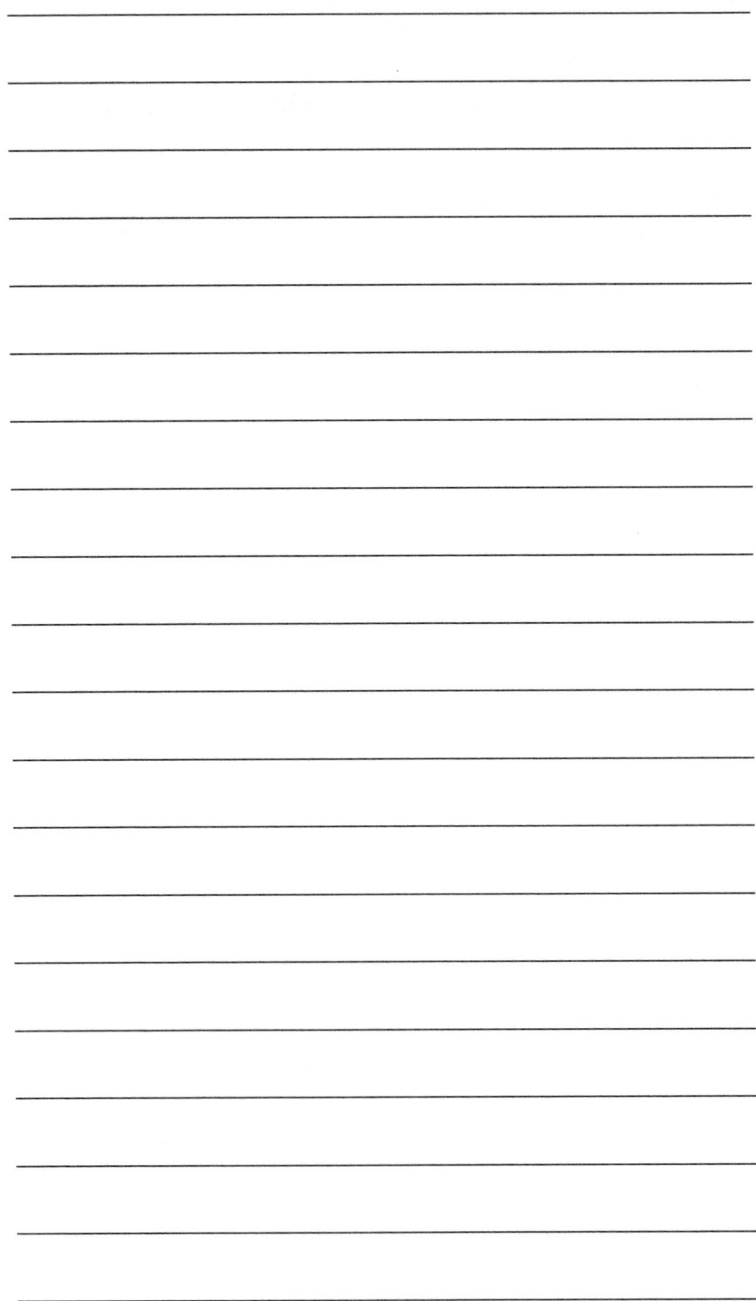

Day 56:

Write down all your bad habits, things about yourself that you don't like, and all the things in your life that you regret. Put them on small pieces of paper – spend time ripping up each one as small as you can and dispense them into the trash. Imagine that every negative thing in your life has just been erased. You have a clean slate, you can start from where you are.

Day 57:

Make a list and learn a couple of yoga poses that you can do without hurting yourself. Try to do these each morning after making your bed, but before having your coffee or breakfast.

_____

_____

_____

_____

_____

_____

_____

_____

_____

_____

_____

_____

_____

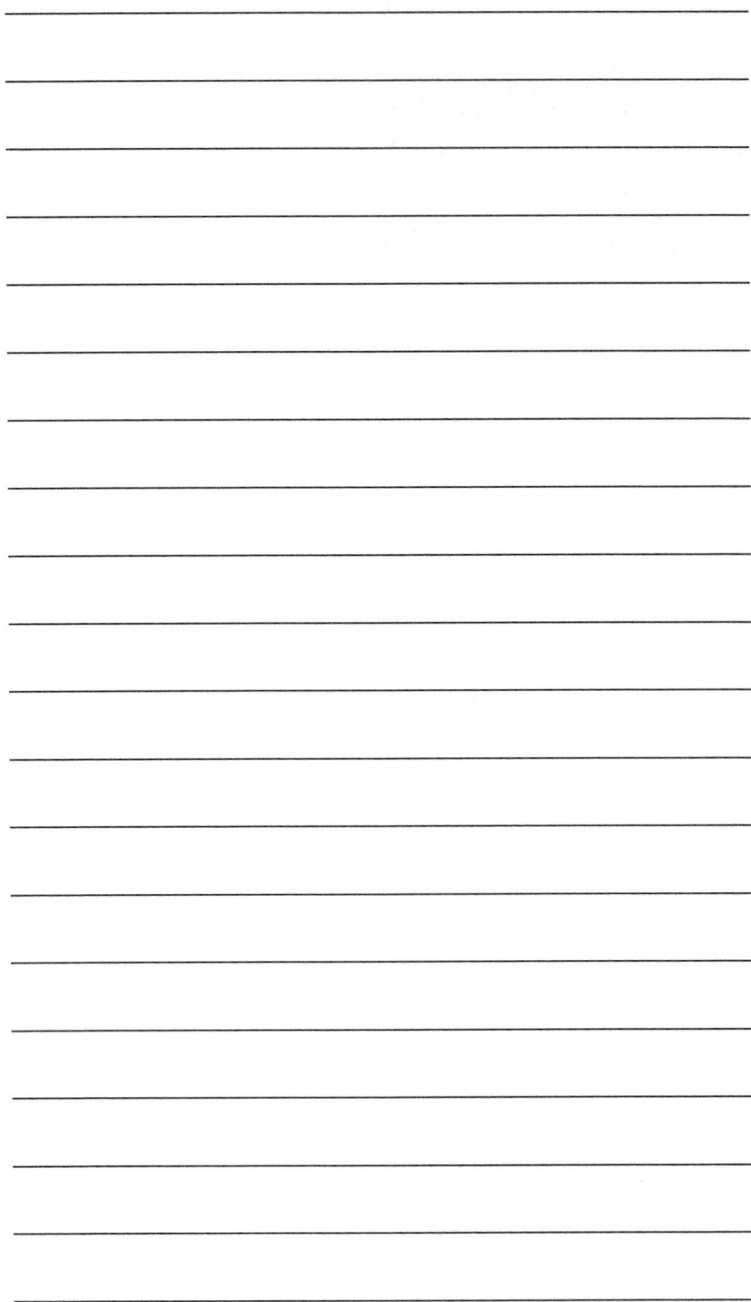

Day 58:

When you go out of your house, say hello to strangers, look people in the eye, smile at them. See if this makes a difference in how people treat you and how you feel – report your findings.

_____

_____

_____

_____

_____

_____

_____

_____

_____

_____

_____

_____

_____

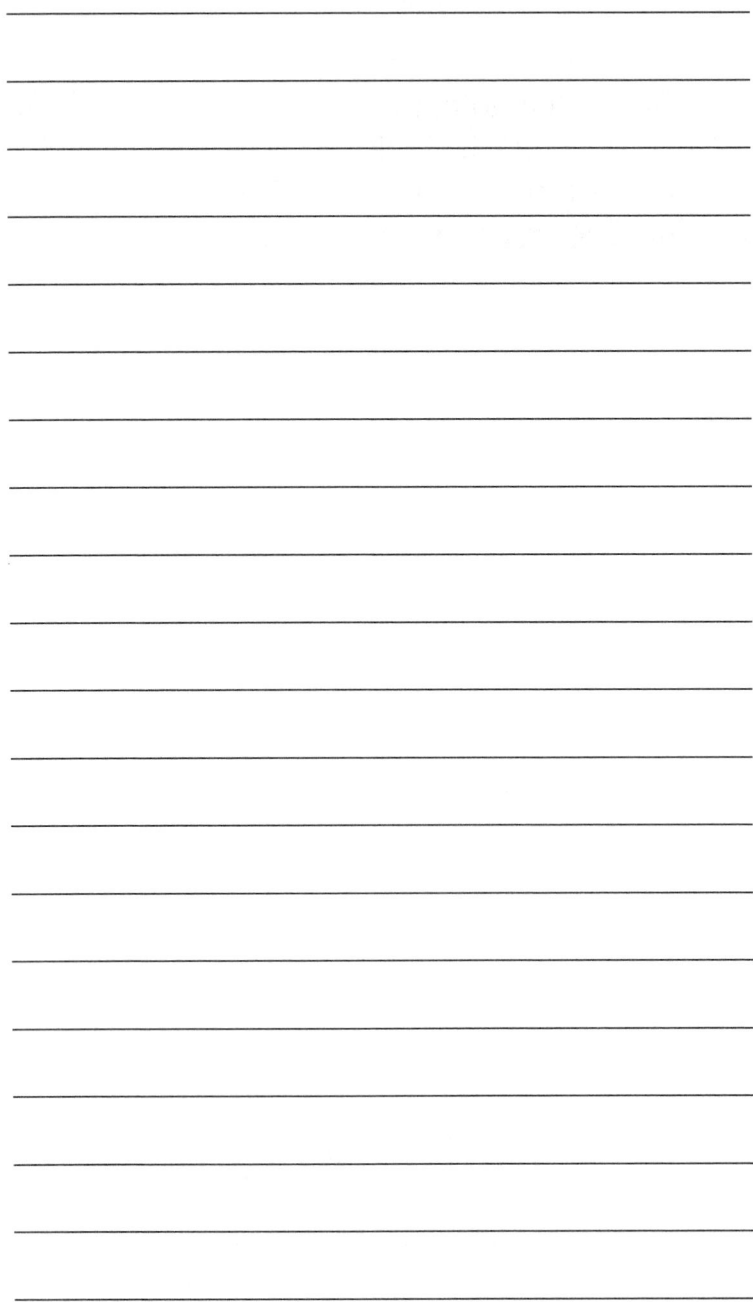

Day 59:

Over the next month, go back over each of these tasks (one or two a day) and add to the ones you can. List the days you added to.

_____

_____

_____

_____

_____

_____

_____

_____

_____

_____

_____

_____

_____

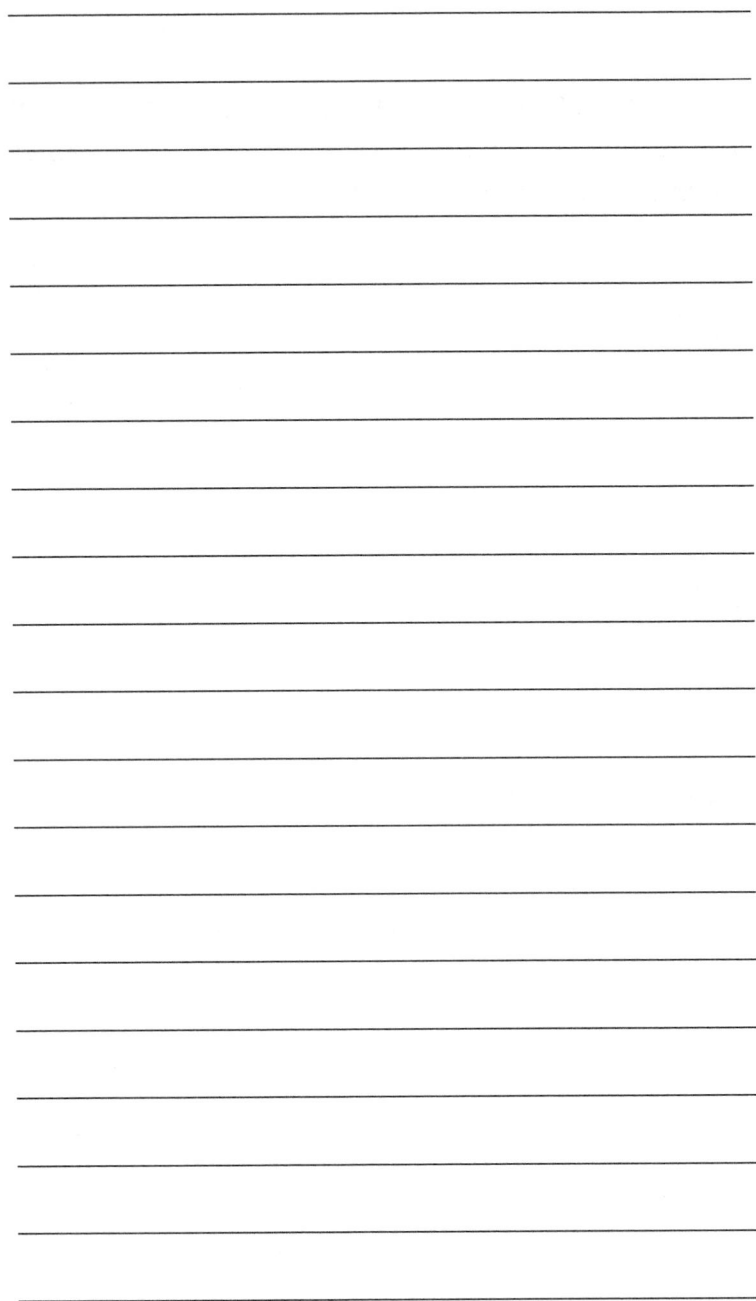

Day 60:

Congratulate yourself for developing a healthy habit. You managed to set aside time every day for 60 days to do a task. Now use the time you used to spend each day on these tasks to starting a journal.

You can write anything! You can keep a journal of your hopes and dreams, you can keep a prayer journal, you can write down your daily moods, you can track your treatment. It is up to you – your imagination is fruitful and you can set the pages on fire!

Write your first journal entry here.

I hope that working through these tasks every day for the past couple months has given you something to concentrate on besides your symptoms, medicine, or any negative circumstances you might be going through – or better yet, maybe it's helped you to work to accept and work through them. I also hope that you've gained a few new skills, remembered to treasure the positive things people have said about you, and discovered some new things that you are good at or that you enjoy.

There is so much that is outside of our control, but feeling good about ourselves is within all of our reach. Having a mental illness is a challenge, but so is being a great human being… you have the skills to handle both!

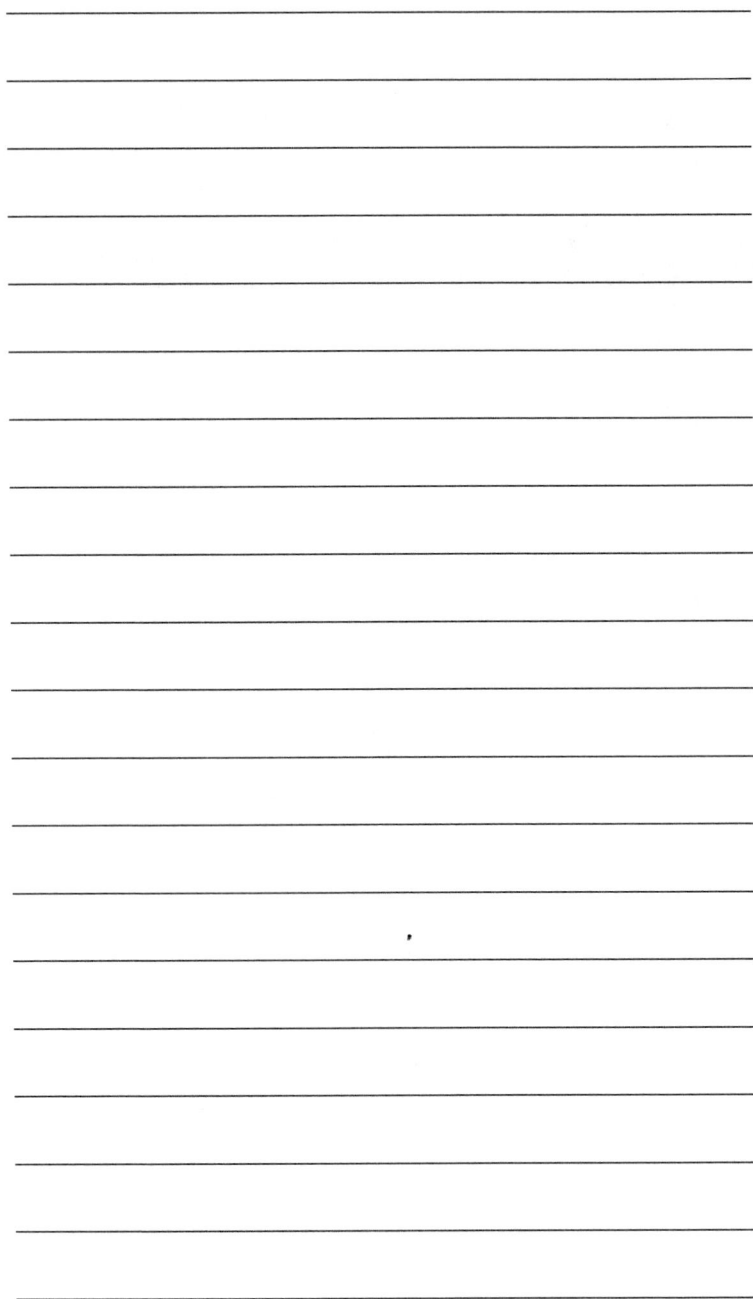

CPSIA information can be obtained
at www.ICGtesting.com
Printed in the USA
BVHW04s0202270918
528564BV00004B/11/P

9 781949 351040